Safed and Keturah

The Third Series of the Parables of Safed the Sage

By William Eleazar Barton

PANTIANOS
CLASSICS

Published by Pantianos Classics

ISBN-13: 978-1-78987-100-5

First published in 1921

Contents

Publishers' Preface (1921)

The popularity of the Parables of Safed the Sage has grown steadily since the appearance of the first of them in the summer of 1915. The Mississippi Mate, whose language was most unlike to that of the pulpit, but whose essential message was not wholly different, introduced this series in that year, and provoked so much of mirth and wholesome reflection that other articles in the same vein followed. The series on the Hollyhocks fairly launched the author upon his career as a grower of those beautiful flowers, bringing him seed from many readers, and requests for seed from the Hollyhocks of Safed.

In some respects this is a unique form of instruction; in others it is very ancient. The things of ordinary life are taken as suggestions for practical lessons. This is a form of instruction not only time-honored, but inevitable. We are continually advancing from the known to the unknown, and interpreting spiritual things in the light of things tangible. But Safed's method is wholly his own. His combination of things new and old is unlike that of any other writer of his generation.

Two volumes of his Parables have already appeared in book form. The third is presented herewith. The publishers are confident that wherever it goes, home life will be more wholesome, childhood will appear more lovable, and common things will be seen to be full of valuable lessons.

The publishers appreciate the interest with which the previous volumes have been welcomed, and are confident that this one will increase the number of those who loved Safed and Keturah.

The Publishers

Introduction

The author of these little chapters thanks the readers, whose interest has been his constant encouragement. The circle has widened considerably since these Parables began to appear. At first they were issued in a single religious newspaper, then in a small group of religious papers, and now they are supposed to be read by not less than three millions of people every week. Safed and Keturah make their modest bow to more people than they at first supposed would probably be interested in them, and express their sincere appreciation of the kind words which reach them now and then through the various editors.

The gathering of this third group of Parables for publication in book form is a pleasant task. With the book the author sends his salutation and best wishes.

No apology is here offered for the optimism which underlies the philosophy of these little lessons. The author has lived long enough to know something of the sorrows and perplexities of life, but he still believes that this is a good world, and he is glad that he is alive and that Keturah is here with him. The two things for which he and Keturah are most thankful are their faith and their friends.

Safed.

Safed and Keturah

The Cherry Pie

Two kinds of women are in the world. And besides these two there is Keturah. The one kind maketh a Cherry Pie and taketh out none of the Stones. The other kind taketh out all of the Stones save one.

Now I climbed the Cherry Tree, I and the Robins, and the Robins climbed higher than I, and got at it earlier and stayed at it later, and I was hard put to it to get any of the Cherries. But some of them I gathered, and I brought them in a Basket, and Keturah put the Kettle on, and certain of them she did Can. But some of them she took, and she made thereof a Cherry Pie.

And the Crust thereof was made so that it did melt in my mouth, and the Cherries were rich with their own juice and with Sugar. And there were plenty of them between the Crusts; for after this manner doth Keturah make Cherry Pie.

And in all the Pie there was not one Cherry Stone. And I knew that it would be so, for Keturah made it.

Now there be women who make Cherry Pies for their husbands, and they say unto them, Behold, here is a Cherry Pie with the Stones in; thou hast more time to Pluck them out than I have; and it is lucky for thee that thou get a Cherry Pie, even with the Stones in; and if thou likest it not, thou canst leave it.

And the other kind say, Behold here is a Cherry Pie, and the Stones thereof have I taken out. But presently her husband biteth hard upon a Stone, and breaketh a Tooth, or crowdeth out a Filling so that it costeth him Four Dollars to Replace it. And when he chideth his wife, she breaketh into tears, and she saith. Thou art a Cruel Man. For thou givest me no credit for the Stones which I took out, and thou blamest me for the one Stone which I overlooked.

Now the Lord hath mercifully spared me that I married neither of those women, but if I had to choose between them, I would take the woman who removeth no Stones from the Cherries, and biddeth her husband to beware, rather than her who professeth to have removed them all, but who leaveth one Stone to insure his weeping and gnashing of teeth.

And the same is true of life, that men can meet bravely many trials when they have reason to expect them, but he is no friend who promiseth Security when there is one hard Bump that a man must come up against, and be unprepared for it.

But take it from me, when Keturah maketh a Cherry Pie, it is some Pie.

7

The Shoes Under the Bed

Of Goodness there be many kinds. For a Shoe becometh good to wear when it becometh bad to look at. Wherefore do I complain when Keturah giveth away any of mine Old Shoes. And Keturah hath provided a place in the Closet, where they may stand in an Orderly Row; but it is my custom when I remove them at night to set them under the edge of the Bed. And at first there is one pair, and then there are other pairs, yea, and a pair of slippers also. And when I arise in the morning, I reach down with mine hand, and take up a Shoe, and if it be not the one that I would wear I set it back and find another.

Now with this System Keturah is not well pleased. Wherefore from time to time doth she gather them up, and set them in array in the Closet. And she saith unto me, Wherefore doth my lord place his shoes under the Bed, which is not Expedient neither Orderly, when he might better place them in a Nice Straight Row in the Closet?

And I said unto her, Thou wast not made as I was made out of the dust of the earth. Thirty and three years ago did God cause a deep sleep to fall upon me. Then took He one of my Ribs and made thee. And thou camest into my life and next to mine heart, not as something from the world without, but as that which already belonged to me, and must be mine so long as the heavens endure. Nevertheless, of all my Ribs art thou the most Unquiet.

And she said, I do admonish thee for thy good.

And I said, O thou fairest among women, were God to establish a school for Husbands, he would make thee Principal. Yea, and I am favored above all men in having become the First and only Graduate of that school, *Magna Cum Laude.*

And Keturah said, Thou hast learned many things, and in much thou hast done well. Yea, and I have yielded the Dipping of the Doughnut in the coffee; why wilt thou not pick up thy shoes?

And I said, If I must, then I needs must.

And I said. Thou hast an Hamper for soiled Clothing, and a Laundry Bag. I will put my Linen in the Laundry Bag, if thou wilt allow me a Little Latitude in the matter of the Shoes.

And Keturah said, For thee that will be doing very well.

And I answered and said, This will I do, even as I have promised, but O Keturah, I do not want to be Reformed any more than I am already Reformed.

And Keturah said, I verily believe that there are worse husbands, even than thou.

And then did she kiss me, which is a way that she hath.

8

The System of Keturah

We sat at a feast, both I and Keturah, and certain others. And the Hostess had prepared a Dinner that was Some Dinner. And we ate thereof and rejoiced. For I enjoy the eating of such Good Things as God hath given to men, and I can eat anything save it be Health Foods.

And the Hostess talked of the Duty of Women to Organize and get their Rights. And she spake right well. And her husband spake not at all.

And the servants brought in the Good Stuff which Cometh toward the end of the Meal, and Keturah took thereof, even of the Ice Cream and of the Cakes. But of the Ice Cream she ate but one small spoonful, and of the cakes brake she off save it were only a Crumb from Each Kind, that she might judge how many Eggs the Recipe called for, and whether they had used Butter or Cotolene.

But as for me, I cared for none of these things, but ate all that was set before me. For I enjoy all manner of sweet things, even Pies and Cakes, and Ice Cream and Conserves, and Apple Pie, and Mince Pie, and Custard Pie, and Cherry Pie whereof all the Stones have been taken out, and Pound Cake, and Sponge Cake, and Cocoanut Cake, and Chocolate Cake, and Angel Cake, and Wedding Cake, and Fruit Cake, and Sherbets and Preserves, and Strawberry Jam, and Apple Butter, and Preserved Figs, and Fruit that hath been preserved in its weight in Sugar, and many other kinds. But Keturah careth little for them; nevertheless she taketh them when I sit nigh unto her.

Now while the Hostess was talking about women Organizing and Having a System, Keturah slipped her Full Plate over to me, and I slipped my empty one back to her, and I ate her Ice Cream, and her Cakes besides mine own. And the Hostess saw it not, neither they that sat at meat.

And this hath Keturah done many times in the years wherein we have been married, and her System worketh to her Complete Satisfaction, yea and to mine.

Now on the next day there came to me a man who said, Behold, I have owed thee Fifty Shekels of long time, and thou didst lend this to me when I was Hard Up. Now will I repay thee.

And I embraced him and I thanked him much; for if all men who have borrowed from me would repay me, I should have more wealth than I now possess.

Now it came to pass that night as we sat at meat that I slipped the Plate of Keturah where mine had been, and mine where hers had been. And she looked, and behold, on the plate which I slipped across to her there were five pieces of gold, each of the value of Ten Shekels.

And she cried out and said, What is this, and whence came it?

And I said. Get thee to the sellers of Silk in the City, and to them that prepare Fine Raiment for women, and buy thee a Stunning New Frock, and see to it thou bring me back No Change.

9

And she asked me saying. Dost thou not need this Money for other things?

And I said, O thou to the arch of whose eyebrow the New Moon is a Servant Maid, some women have a System different from thine, but thine Suiteth me Mighty Well, and from time to time there shall be Reciprocity. I also will work thy system and see how well it worketh in Reverse Gear.

And I thought of men whose Religion consisteth in Teasing God for what they think are their Rights or their Desires, and others who delight in giving to God the best that they have. And I said in mine heart that those Christians get most out of the Goodness of God who follow the system of Keturah. For it is a system that worketh well both with man and God.

The Sunny Side of the Street

Now the Shears wherewith I write much of my wisdom became Dull, so that they would not cut easily. And I looked out of my Window and I saw on the other side of the Street an Ancient man out of Denmark, who goeth to and fro, and sharpeneth Knives and Shears and Repaireth Things. And I went to him, and I besought him, saying. Come thou and sharpen my Shears.

And he said, It is morning now, and thou livest on the East Side of the Street; therefore will I come not now, but I will come when it is toward Evening.

But I said, I shall not be there when it is toward evening. Come thou now.

And as he sharpened my Shears, I asked him, saying. Why didst thou refuse to come to me in the Morning?

And he said, All living things require the Sun. The trees grow not save they have the sun, and no life thrives if it have it not. Therefore do I always go on the West side of the Street in the morning, and on the East side in the Evening.

And he said. Thou art a man of Learning. Behold, I would speak to thee of many things.

And he opened a Box that he carried, and he took out a Tray wherein were his Tools, and beneath the Tray were Books that he was Reading, yea, and a Book that he was Writing. And he read to me out of the book. And it had in it many strange Theories, and Interesting Ideas. And although I did not think them Sound, yet I marveled that this Commonplace Ancient Man of Denmark thought of the Deep Things of Life as he Sharpened his Knives and Scissors.

Now it had been hard for me to get him to come to me in the morning, because I lived on the East Side of the Street, but it was harder to get him to leave before Evening,' because he had many things to talk about, and he cared much more to talk about them than he did to Sharpen Shears. Nevertheless, he left me.

And I spake unto Keturah, and I said. That old Dane hath many a Strange Bat in his Belfry, but he hath some notions that are not Half Bad. Human life hath One Road, whereon all men travel, and they travel every man in one and the Same Direction. For at one end of the road is the Cradle, and at the other end thereof there is the Grave, and there be no man who travels that road backward. But although the Road hath but one Direction yet hath it Two Sides. Therefore will I shout to all men who travel the Highway of Life, and I will say unto them, Walk ye on the Sunny Side.

The Spliced String

There came to me a man who had made no great success of his own affairs, but who was eloquent as to methods whereby other men might Win Success. And his great god whereby he swore was named Efficiency.

And he spake unto me, saying. The trouble with the Churches, and with the Whole Shooting Match of thy kind of work, is that it knoweth nothing of Efficiency.

And I answered and said unto him,

The home of my boyhood had in it no Fireplace, but we bought our String by the Ball. And the home of my Grandsire had a Vast Fireplace, but they bought no String, for they kept the twine that came wrapped around packages from the store. Wherefore in mine own home if I desired a String, I went to the ball, and cut off how much soever I would. But in the house of my Grandsire if I asked for String, my Grandmother did give me a little piece that had come to her with the Sugar or the Starch. Now there was a day when I was in the home of my Grandsire, and I desired a long String. And I besought my Grandmother, and she gave me Many Short Strings. And I began to tie them together, and to lay out the long string that I was making on the Floor, that I might discern how long it was. And I began at the end of the room that was next unto the Fireplace. And when I had laid down my first string, and tied another to the end of it, I stopped to untangle another string.

Then did a Spark fly out from the Fireplace and light the end of my string. And I knew it not. But I went to the end of the room, and I passed through the door into the next Room, and I tied on more string. And behold, the fire followed me as fast as I tied, and when I looked around, I had but one string, and that was shorter than any one of those that I had tied together. Even so is it with thine Efficiency. He is a god with feet of clay that cannot bear up his own weight, and he burneth up practical results faster than he tieth on his new methods.

And the man said. Thou dost not understand. Be silent and I will explain to thee the workings of Efficiency.

And I said. The greater part of thine efficiency is like unto a Steamboat with a Small Boiler and a Big Whistle. Whenever it bloweth the Whistle the Engine stoppeth, and it bloweth the Whistle continually.

And he saw that I was Hopeless, and he left me.

Of Knowing Too Little and Too Much

There came to the City wherein I dwell a man who delivered a Lecture, and I and Keturah we went. And the subject whereof he spake was one about which he knew very little. But he spread that little over the surface of an Interesting Talk, and the people enjoyed it, and so did we. Yea, and we were profited thereby, although the Lecturer knew little more than he told us.

And there came another man who spake on the same subject, and we went to hear him. And he was a man of Great Erudition. And I said. Now shall we hear something Worth While.

But he began by telling us the History of the Subject and the Various Attempts to Elucidate it. And then he spake of the Various Theories that had been Suggested concerning it, and the books that had been written in Divers Tongues with regard to it. And he said that a certain opinion had been held by men of learning, but was now no longer highly regarded, but that the opinion that was to take its place was in dispute. And he suggested Various Aspects of the theme which he said he could not Discuss because it would require a Volume on any one of them.

And about that time it was time to stop, and he stopped.

And as we journeyed toward our home, Keturah said, He certainly is a man of large knowledge.

And I answered. Yea, and for the purposes of that audience it were better if he had known the tenth part of what he knoweth. For the first man carried all his goods in his show window, and this man blocked the sidewalk with dray-loads of unopened cases and bales of unassimilable and useless wisdom.

And Keturah said, I have heard that a Little Knowledge is a Dangerous thing.

And I said. Believe it not. A little knowledge is good for seed, but there is such a thing as that a man getteth drowned in his own knowledge. For the first man knew little, but used that little effectively, and the second man knew much, and it was useless.

And I said unto Keturah, Like unto a Spider that is entangled in its own web, so is the man of much knowledge who is unable to employ it. Better is it that a man know little and be able to use it wisely, than to know much and to get lost in the swamp of it.

And Keturah said, Nevertheless, I think that knowledge is good, and much knowledge is better than little.

And I said. All human knowledge is small, and the difference between the man who knoweth much and the man who knoweth little is too small to waste much time in futile distinctions. For in the sight of God the wisdom of both is foolishness. But the value of knowledge is in the use of it.

And Keturah inquired of me, saying, Art thou a man of much knowledge or of little?

And I answered, If so be that I am able to use my knowledge and get away with it, what doth it matter if it be little or large? Behold, though I be ignorant, yet have I no trouble in finding people yet more ignorant, and if the stream wherein they swim is over their head, what doth it matter if it be an inch or ten thousand cubits?

And Keturah said, I do verily believe that among the ignorant men of earth there be some who are more ignorant than my lord; and if any of them do think thee wise, I shall not tell them that it is not so.

And I said, A little honey on the end of a rod was nigh unto being the death of Jonathan, but it enlightened his eyes, and it was better than an whole bee-hive whereof one might see only the outside.

The Stone Half Way Up

There came unto me one of the great men in Israel, upon whom God had laid the burden of a Great Task. And he said unto me, Safed, art thou ever Weary?

And I answered him, saying. Well, hardly ever.

And he inquired of me again, saying, Art thou ever Completely Discouraged?

And I answered him, I have ever one more Shot in my Locker.

And he said, I am Completely Tired Out; and what is worse, I am Discouraged.

And I said unto him, O my friend, God hath highly honored thee in giving to thee a Task beyond thy Strength. Listen to the word of a wise man, who thus spake unto me. Seek not for tasks to which thy strength is equal; seek rather for strength adequate to thy tasks.

And he said, Yea, but this is Up-Hill all the way.

And I said, There is no Hill that reached to the sky, and every Hill hath beyond its Summit a Down-Hill Side. If thou stop now, half way up, thy task shall roll back upon thee and crush thee; but if thou put a little more Punch into thine Up-Hill Rolling of the Stone, then shalt thou come to the Crest, and the thing will roll more easily downward.

And he said, I know that it is so, but I fear that this task will kill me.

And I laughed him to scorn, and I said, Take courage; for thou shalt yet dance upon the Coffin-lid of this job.

And as he rose to go, I said unto him. Listen, O my friend, and mark well my words. Some men when they die will be Dust; but by the grace of God it shall not be so with me nor yet with thee. We shall not be Dust, but Ashes.

The Millionaire and the Scrublady

There is a certain Millionaire, who hath his Offices on the Second Floor of the First National Bank Building. And when he goeth up to his Offices he rideth in the Elevator, but when he goeth down, then he walketh.

And he is an Haughty Man, who once was poor, and hath risen in the World, and he is a Self-made Man who worshipeth his maker.

And he payeth his Rent regularly on the first day of the month, and he considereth not that there are Human Beings who run the Elevators, and who Clean the Windows, hanging at a great height above the Sidewalk, and who shovel Coal into the furnaces under the Boilers. Neither doth he at Christmas time remember any of them with a Tip or a Turkey.

And there is in that Building a Poor Woman who Scrubbeth the Stairs and the Halls. And he hath walked past her often but hath never seen her until Recently. For his head was high in the air, and he was thinking of More Millions.

Now it came to pass on a day that he left his Office, and started to walk down the Stairs.

And the Scrublady was half way down; for she had begun at the top, and was giving the stairs their First Onceover. And upon the topmost Stair, in a wet and soapy spot, there was a Large Cake of Yellow Soap. And the Millionaire stepped upon it.

Now the foot which he set upon the Soap flew eastward toward the Sunrise, and the other foot started on an expedition of its own toward the going down of the Sun. And the Millionaire sat down upon the Topmost Step, but he did not remain there. As it had been his Intention to Descend, so he Descended, but not in the manner of his Original Design. For he descended faster, and he struck each step with a sound as it had been of a Drum.

And the Scrublady stood aside courteously, and let him go. And he stayed not on the order of his going.

And at the bottom he arose, and considered whether he should rush into the Office of the Building and demand that the Scrublady be fired; but he considered that if he should tell the reason there would be great Mirth among the occupants of the Building. And so he held his peace.

But since that day he taketh notice of the Scrublady, and passeth her with Circumspection.

For there is no man so high or mighty that he can afford to ignore any of his fellow human beings. For a very Humble Scrublady and a very common bar of Yellow Soap can take the mind of a Great Man off his Business Troubles with surprising rapidity.

Wherefore, consider these things, and count not thyself too high above even the humblest of the children of God.

Lest haply thou come down from thy place of pride and walk off with thy bruises aching a little more by reason of thy suspicion that the Scrublady is

Smiling into her Suds, and facing the day's work the more cheerfully by reason of the fun thou hast afforded her.

For these are solemn days, and he that bringeth a smile to the face of a Scrublady hath not lived in vain.

The Long Walk

The daughter of the daughter of Keturah hath a little friend who cometh to see her, and playeth with her in the Yard, hard by the Window, where their voices may be heard inside the House. And mostly they play very Happily; but now and then for the sake of Variety they indulge in Argument and Comparison like grown Folk. And it was upon a day that they got thus into a Friendly Scrap, the first part of which I heard not. But the Argument had reached a stage where the daughter of the daughter of Keturah was advancing and backing the other little damsel off the Map, and the other little girl could only answer, I did not, or You can not, or It is not.

And the daughter of the daughter of Keturah said,

I can walk Fifty-nine miles.

And the other little girl said. You can not.

And the daughter of the daughter of Keturah said, I can take my Grandpa's hand and keep up with him, and he can walk Fifty-nine miles, and I can walk Fifty-nine miles with' him if I hold his hand.

And the other little damsel said, You can not.

Then did the daughter of the daughter of Keturah tell unto the other little girl how great and good a Grandpa she had. And I am too modest a man to write down what she said; but if George Washington and Solomon and a few others were to live in one, peradventure he might be a Second-cousin or a Remote Acquaintance of a man such as the daughter of the daughter of Keturah described.

And the other little girl was speechless; for she could not say. Thy grandpa is not the only Pebble on the Beach; I also have a Grandpa whose hair is fully as Grey and whose Bald Spot is larger than thy Grandpa's; for the daughter of the daughter of Keturah had carried the matter beyond all comparison. And the other little girl could only change the subject, and say,

I can kick your whole house down and all your trees.

And the daughter of the daughter of Keturah, knowing that she had won out, said sweetly,

Go ahead.

Now there is no man who knoweth so well as I how far from right is the estimate of the little maiden concerning the goodness and the greatness of her Grandpa. Nevertheless it pleased me more than any man can understand who is not a Grandpa; for unto none others hath the Lord given wisdom to know of such matters. And the next time a man goeth by and bloweth a small whistle, she shall have a Red Balloon.

For apart from her beautiful delusion concerning the poor man concerning whom I pray my God that she may be never undeceived, the little maiden is not wholly wrong. For when she holdeth my hand she can do things which otherwise she could not do.

And I prayed unto my God a prayer, and I said,

O my God, Thou hast permitted us through the gift of little lives such as these to discern spiritual truths which thou hast hid from the wise and prudent and revealed unto babes, that so we might enter into the Kingdom of Heaven as little children. Grant unto me this, O my Father, that I shall hold so fast to Thine Hand that the journey that would otherwise be impossible shall be possible for me, and the task that would have been too great may be accomplished through thy strength. For I can do all things through Him that strengtheneth me and if I hold Thy Hand I can run and not be weary, and walk and not faint.

The Pet Aversions

We went unto a Reception, I and Keturah. And when they gave unto us Sandwiches and a Cup of Tea, and nowhere to set it, there came a woman and sat beside me. And she inquired of me, saying. Art thou Safed the Sage?

And I answered, I am Safed; and concerning my sagacity there is an honest difference of opinion.

And she said, I have somewhat against thee, for my husband hath read thy Stuff, and he telleth me that thou hast no love for Curl Papers. . And since he hath read thy Parables, he scoldeth me for wearing a Boudoir Cap to breakfast. But if I did not wear it in the morning, how should my hair look nice for the Reception?

And I said unto her, I have three pet aversions, yea, four things do I abhor. They are bedclothes that come out at the foot, and Tapioca Pudding, and Fringed White Napkins for a man who weareth a Black Coat, and Curl Papers at breakfast.

And she said, But is not the Boudoir Cap all right?

And I said, The Lord hath given unto me a mighty spirit of discernment so that I behold under its lace and ribbon a frowsled head and untidy Curl Papers.

And she said, A woman desireth to look her best when she goeth out.

And I said, A woman should try as hard to look well in the sight of her husband as she did before he was her husband.

And I got her a second cup of tea, and departed.

And as we went our way, Keturah said, I beheld thee in conversation with such and such a lady. How didst thou like her?

And I said unto Keturah, If that woman should discover the list of women whom I have selected for my second wife, she might read it, softly humming. Is My Name Written There? and she would seek it in vain.

And Keturah said, May I read that list?

And I said, I will typewrite it for thee and paste it upon thy Mirror.

And the list that I pasted there had these names and no more:

Keturah.

Keturah.

Keturah.

And Keturah said, Though I commend thy good taste in desiring that thy first wife be also thy second, and I feel duly honored, yet am I not sure that I will marry as my second husband a man who giveth no better reason for choosing me than that I do not wear a Boudoir Cap to breakfast. And I said, That may not be my only reason, but it is a sufficient reason to a man who desireth a few Pet Prejudices, such as mine against the Boudoir Cap at breakfast. There be women who nag their husbands, and women who season the coffee of their husbands with Rough on Rats, and I desire none of them. But I would rather marry both Xantippe and Lucretia Borgia than a woman who doth not comb her hair until after breakfast. Yea, rather than that thou shouldest come down to breakfast with a Boudoir Cap hiding Curl Papers, I would see thee Chew Gum in Prayer Meeting.

Things That Are Small

I was putting on my Outer Garments, and going unto a Committee Meeting. And I was late. And Keturah said unto me. Go thou by the way of the house of our Daughter, and give unto her this Package, and speak unto her such and such Messages, and then go thou unto thy Committee Meeting.

And I did even as she said unto me. But I was in haste, and I tarried not long, nor sat down.

And as I hastened away, I heard a great Cry, and I turned back to see if the daughter of the daughter of Keturah had broken her Neck. And she had not broken her Neck, but I had broken her Heart.

And I asked. What is the matter with my little girl?

And she sobbed and she answered. Grandpa hardly spoke to me. I am so little he does not care for me.

Now when I heard this I was smitten to mine heart, for it had been even as she said. And the little maiden is unto me as the Apple of mine Eye. But I had been in an Hurry, for there was a Committee Meeting, and I was late.

And I entered the House, and I took her into mine arms, and I sat in a Chair with the little maiden in my lap, and with her Golden Hair upon my Shoulder, and I said. Let the Committee Meeting go hang.

And she said, You do love me. Grandpa, don't you, even if I am small?

And I said. My dear, I love thee as much as if thou wert the Fat Lady in the Side Show, and maybe more. Yea, I do not think it would be possible for a Grandsire to love a little damsel more than I love thee.

And she put her arms around my neck, and the Committee Meeting just had to mosey along as best it could till I got there.

Now after a while she got down, and we bade each other an Happy Good-bye, and I went my way. And as I went, I thought of the children of God who sometimes get to feeling just the same way, and thinking that their Heavenly Father doth not care for them because they are so Little, and He is busy with Great Things.

And I prayed unto my God on behalf of all such Heart-Broken children of His, that He will gather them in his arms, and comfort them, and tell them to cast all their care upon Him, for it Mattereth to Him concerning them.

Asking And Receiving

I have a friend and he hath an Automobile; and as I climbed in beside him upon the front seat he remarked,

The Automobile hath become a necessity.

And I answered him and said. Yea, verily: it is necessary for me that my friends shall own them.

And we had a fine ride. For I have an half ownership in the Cars of all my friends. And they are mighty good to me.

And we rode afar. And behold there stood upon the Curb a lad who looked as if he would go somewhere. And my friend slowed down, for he said,

Behold, that lad desireth to go in our direction, and we will take him in on the back seat and help him on his journey.

And as we drew nigh and slowed down the lad yelled,

Gimme a ride.

And he prepared to climb in.

But my friend stepped on the gas and the car shot forward, and left the lad upon the curb.

And my friend said.

It maketh me all fired mad the manners of this rising generation. That lad was well dressed, and the folk in this part of town are good families; and he should know how to address a gentleman and how to ask a Favour. But he knoweth nothing save to make an Impudent Demand. Yea, it is so with most of them. Politeness to older folk is unknown to them. The kids of this generation are the limit.

Now I considered this matter and I resolved that I would say to the young folk of this generation that Politeness costeth very little and often helpeth one on his journey, while Impudence getteth a man nowhere. And I resolved that I would suggest to them that they learn to say, If thou dost please, and also, I thank thee.

Then I considered those who ask of God and receive not because they ask amiss. And I wondered if God doth not speed up the Universe and leave some men standing on the curb because they have not yet learned to be Polite unto God.

The Late Arrival

There liveth in a certain city a man whose name is John Smith, and he hath been for many years an Honest and Inconspicuous Citizen. And it came to pass after many years that his name began to appear Among Those Present; and it seemed unto him Mighty Good to get into the outer edges of the Limelight, and he began to yearn for a place a little nearer unto the Center of the Stage.

Now there was a great Public Banquet at the leading Hotel, and all the Prominent Citizens shook their Dress Suits out from the Moth Balls and were present. And John Smith had a place at the Further End of the Speakers' Table.

And after the Hoi Polloi were seated, then did the Occupants of the Speakers' Table file in and take their seats, while the Band played. It Looketh unto me like a Big Night Tonight. And John Smith felt good clean down into his Boots to think that a Part of that Chautauqua Salute was for him.

Now there was one Vacant Seat at the Speakers' Table, and they all knew whose it was. For G. Fred Jones did habitually arrive late. And when he came in about twelve minutes after all the others were seated, then did the Band play, Hail to the Chief. And the Presiding Officer walked over and said. So good of thee to come; we feared that thou hadst been detained.

Now John Smith believed all this, and he said: I am wise to this little Game. It is he who cometh late that getteth the Glad Hand, whereas he who cometh in with the Bunch is unnoticed.

Now there came another Banquet and John Smith had a seat a little further from the end and a little nearer to the center of the Speakers' Table, and he arrived fifteen minutes late. And he said: Now for the Big Noise when I enter.

And behold, as he drew nigh, he heard the sound of Music, for the Band was playing. Hail, Hail, the Gang's All Here, and he slipped in wholly unobserved.

When he sought for his seat, behold it had been given unto another, for the Presiding Officer said: We thought thou wert out of Town. Now behold, there are some good seats yonder by the Door. Go thou away back and be thou seated.

And he went away back and sat down. And he did not enjoy the Banquet a little bit, neither did his food that he ate that night agree with him and his applause of the Speeches lacked something of Heartiness.

And he said within himself: Behold, I have several times made of myself a Fool, but this is the worst in all my sweet young life. For I perceive that he who setteth his foot upon the First Round of the Ladder of Publick Recognition, is a Fool if he thinketh that he hath already attained. For he who hath arrived can work those little stunts that increase his Popularity, whereas if a man more obscure doth attempt one of them, he only increaseth his obscurity.

And I considered this Truthful Tale, and I said: Little Fishes Should Keep nigh unto the Shore. Nevertheless there is yet hope for John Smith, for he is capable of learning Wisdom from his own Folly, and that is the only real way in Which Wise Men such as I have attained Wisdom. For we all started with a Large Endowment of Folly, and it departeth very slowly from even the Wisest of Men.

The Iron Fetters

I rode upon a Train; and the day drew on toward Evening, and the Porter came to make down my Berth. And I sat for a time in the next section, where was a man and a young man. And the Man said. Sit here if thou wilt. And he moved over. And when I sat down, behold, there was something hard under me. And I Essayed to remove it, but I saw what it was, and I pushed it into the Corner of the Seat, for I did not desire to publish unto the people of the Car what I had found. And I said unto the man, I am not very familiar with this kind of Ornament.

And he said. It belongeth unto me.

And we talked of other things. But I saw the young man's ankles that they were bound with an heavy strap, so that he might walk a little in the Car, but take short steps only. So that not every one noticed that he was bound with Fetters.

And in the Night I heard in the berth that was next to mine the Clank of the Fetters. For the Sheriff took off the strap and placed the iron fetter upon the ankle of the lad, one fetter upon the lad's ankle, and one upon his own. And this had they done for Four Nights. Even all the way from Seattle to Syracuse.

And I listened unto the clank of the Fetters, and it grieved me that it should be so. And I considered that he that bindeth his fellow man is bound with him; and the Keeper of a Prison is himself a Prisoner; and the fetters of iron wherewith a man may manacle another man bind him also.

Now in the evening I had not spoken unto the young man of his bonds. Neither did I let him see that I had noticed him. But in the morning the Sheriff spake unto me, and he said,

This young man and I have slept for four nights in the same berth, bound foot to foot, and neither of us have slept any too well. And last night we spake of thee: and I said unto him, I think that he is a man of God. And now, behold, the lad desireth to speak unto thee. And it may be that thou canst say good things unto him. For we have come from the Coast, and we get off at Syracuse, and then he goeth to jail to await his Trial.

So I sat with the young man, and I asked him no questions, but he told me many things. And the Burden of it all was this,

I have a good Father, but I thought he was too strict with me, and a good Mother, but I thought she was an Old Fogy. And I loved the Bright Lights and the Praise of the Gang. And I saw in the Movies how easily one might be Rich, and I wanted some Easy Coin. Therefore have they brought me back twenty-five hundred miles for Grand Larceny.

And I spake unto him such words as God gave unto me. And I said, Think not that the chain of iron upon thy feet is thy worst Fetter. For behold, thou wast chained already when thou didst covet that which was not thine own: and in throwing off the yoke of thy father and the advice of thy mother, thou didst become the Prisoner of Evil.

And he said, Verily, I know it.

And the Sheriff said. He is not a bad kid at heart: but thus is it with the man that despiseth the law of his father and disregardeth the tears of his mother.

Now the train reached Syracuse and there was a Patrol Wagon backed up at the Curb. And I said unto the young man.

Tell the truth, whatever it shall cost thee.

Take thy medicine, however so bitter it may be. Beware of evil companions. Seek forgiveness and help from thy God. And see that thou die not until thou make thy mother proud of thee.

And he asked me for my name, and the name of the City where I dwelt. And he said, One day I shall come to see thee; and then shall be no bracelets on my wrists, neither straps nor irons on my legs, but I shall be honest and free.

And I said unto him, If the Son of God shall make thee free, thou shalt be free indeed.

The Great Game

I journeyed by Boat in the Good Old Summertime; and I put off my Prophet's Mantle, and I wore a Short Coat and a Cap and I looked like a Minister off on his Vacation save that I Draw the Line at a Red Necktie. And the Ship's Clock struck Five Bells, which meaneth Half Past Six. So I went unto the Dining Room, and the Head Steward gave me a place at a Table where Three People already were seated. And one of them was a Lady, and she sat Over Against me.

And she sought to put me at my ease at once, and to make me a Member of the Party. And she Spake unto her Husband, but she looked at me, and she said:

Now this is Very Pleasant to have this Fourth Place filled, for I never like to sit at a Table with a Vacant Place across from me. And I am sure we welcome this Gentleman to our Little Group. And, furthermore, I am persuaded that he is a Good Bridge Player. And after we have Dined we may sit in the Aft Cabin and play a Pleasant Little Game.

And her Husband, being thus admonished to Follow her Lead, addressed me, saying, Welcome to Our City.

And we spake of the Weather, and How Much Better it was to travel by Boat than by Rail in Hot Weather, and how it was a Calm Night. And then the Lady Resumed the Subject of Bridge. And she said.

Tell me, am I not Right? I know a Good Bridge Player every time. And this also have I observed, that all Really Good Bridge Players Deny It.

Now if I had admitted it she would have felt sure she was right, and if I had denied it she would have felt more sure. Therefore, I held my peace, and spake of other things.

But again she asked me, and I said, I play a more serious game.

And she said, Oh, I know! You men all think Poker is so much better than Bridge! But Poker is a Man's Game and I like it not. But I just love Bridge;

And I said, The Apostle Paul speaketh of Epaphroditus that he played the Gambler with his life for the Lord's sake. And he commendeth his associates as Men who had Hazarded their lives for the Kingdom of God. I play the Great Game of Life, face to face with an inscrutable player whose Hand is hidden so that I see not the cards she holdeth. And some men call her Nature, and some men Fate or Destiny, but the servant of God playeth ever in the darkness with an Angel that will not tell its name. And the hazard is this, that in a world where many of the Cards are black and some are red, I wager my very soul that Hearts are trumps. I play the Game of Life with all that I possess staked on my belief that, though Money driveth men mad, the Diamond and all that it representeth doth not take the trick; that in a world where Cruelty doth abound, and War doth rage, and Death doth walk abroad, the Spade is not the card that winneth all things upon the green table of the earth. I stake mine all upon my faith that Hearts are trumps, and that Love is the highest card in the pack. I bet my life that Love is after all the Greatest thing in the world. That God is love, and men are brothers, and that at the end of the Game when we all Cash In we shall find that he who said that Diamonds were trumps will go where his Money will purchase nothing, and he who hath said that Clubs were trumps will go where clubs and cannon count for nothing, and he who hath said that Spades were trumps will find that Death is not a finality, but Life and Love and God and Duty and Heroism and Sacrifice Win Out. That is the Great Game which I play. And the Stakes are High. I have Bet my Life as Epaphroditus did, and have hazarded my soul like the three men in the Burning Fiery Furnace. I have made my wager that God is good, and Love is the final law of the universe.

And I ceased, and the Lady said,

Oh, I just *do love* to hear you talk! Oh, I think it's *just grand* to be able to talk like that!

And of Bridge spake they no more.

The Ship That Did Not Sail

He who rideth on a railway train in hot weather when he might go by boat should be condemned with this awful condemnation, to wit, that he should be permitted to ride upon a railway train. For this was the condemnation of Judas that he went to his Own Place; so can no sinner ever go to any Hell save he doth carry his own Brimstone with him.

There was a day when Keturah and I sat both of us together upon the Deck of a Ship and we paid the fare and we said: Tonight we go from Boston to Portland.

And I spake to Keturah and said, Seest thou these three ships? They all leave at Six o'clock, and the one over against us goes to New York. We shall behold a Grand Sight when all three leave the dock together.

And Keturah said. Where doth the one ahead of us go?

And I answered, I know not. But it must leave in order that we may leave. For its stern overlappeth our bow; and because it is now nigh unto six o'clock the ship cannot well leave before that. Therefore know I that the three ships must leave at once.

But I was mistaken.

The ship whose stern did overlap our bow was Not Going Anywhere. The ship for New York did leave promptly at six o'clock and ours began to get ready to leave at six. But the ship that was Not Going Anywhere merely slacked her Cables and pulled ahead Six Fathoms or Something like that, and Barely let us out. And by the time our ship was out in the stream the New York Boat was Two Knots down the Harbor and Going Some, and we were Not In It with her. Our ship left the Dock in Isolation.

Now I spake of this to Keturah, saying. The Church hath great enterprises which call for the Launching of Great Fleets in which many Christians sail abreast, but every now and then it Cometh to pass that some Sleepy Christian who Isn't Going Anywhere, unless it may be to Heaven, and who is Mighty Slow even about that, lieth Moored to the Dock, Fore and Aft, bound Bow and Stern with Cables of Tradition or Habit or Inertia, and not only Spreadeth not his own Sails, but lieth athwart the course of his Fellow Christians till the opportunity is Just Disappearing over the Horizon, and even then he barely maketh Grudging Room for some one else to make a Futile and Belated Start. When they fail he sayeth, I told you so.

And I wish that the Christians who do not Go Anywhere would go To Heaven or Somewhere, and Let Other People Do Things.

Something Different

I walked In the Garden, I and the daughter of the daughter of Keturah. And the Garden was bright with the colors of the Spring, like Eden in the day when God made man. And if there were any Snakes there, I and the daughter of the daughter of Keturah beheld them not.

And the little damsel plucked a Flower, and she said, Grandpa, stoop down.

And I stooped down. And she placed the Flower in the Buttonhole of my Coat.

And she said. That is because I love you.

And we went into the house, and Keturah greeted us, and I would have passed into mine own part of the house. But the daughter of the daughter of Keturah constrained me. And she said. Grandma, don't you see the Difference?

And Keturah said, I see that thy Grandsire hath a flower which he had not when he went out into the Garden.

And the little maiden said, I put it there.

And she knew in her heart that she had wrought a good deed, and that she had brightened the day.

And I looked at the Flower, and I said, I also see the Difference. A man with a flower in his Buttonhole hath something to live up to. The dear Lord Christ said unto his disciples, Consider the Lilies; and the lilies were not the only flowers that He loved. And who knoweth that He desired his disciples to consider them only when they were in the Field, and not when they were in the Buttonhole? Even the king is served by the Field, and the Field is for the Buttonhole and for the residue of human need.

Now I considered the Flower which the little girl had given me, and I meditated on the words which she had spoken unto Keturah. And I tried to be particularly good unto Keturah that day, and I asked of her, saying. Dost thou not see the Difference?

And I sought out a high place where I could speak unto the sons of men, and I said unto them.

Oh, ye men, yea, and ye women also. Hearken unto me, and consider the Difference. If thou shalt place in thy Buttonhole one Flower, and wear it until it fadeth, thou shalt by so much brighten the day for many people before the blossom falleth. And if thou shalt do for thy fellow man one kind deed that sendeth him away with a little joy in his heart, thou shalt brighten for him many days, even so many as those in which he remembereth thy kindness. In time when men are depressed by the High Cost of Living and the Difficulties of the Freight Situation and the Fear of Panic; and in times when Pestilence walketh abroad, and every man talketh to his neighbor about the Flu or some other Disease of men's bodies or minds, wear thou a Flower in thy Buttonhole, and a Smile on thy Face and a Song in thy Heart. So shall no evil befall thee, nor any plague come nigh thy dwelling, and thou shalt be one of God's messengers unto others. For men will notice the Difference.

And if so be that the Flower is placed there by any little maiden like unto the daughter of the daughter of Keturah, then shalt thou also notice a Difference. For she maketh a Very Important Difference.

The Moving Vehicles

I rode in a Railway Train, and it was late at a Junction where I changed Cars. And a man rode with me and changed at the same place. And we got out of one train and into another and were quick about it. And he said unto me, For a man of thine age, thou leavest and boardest a train with agility.

And he asked. What is thine Occupation?

And I answered and said, I am employed in jumping on and off Moving Vehicles, such as Cabs and Taxis and Automobiles and such like.

And he said, In what Race dost thou perform these Stunts?

And I said, The Human Race.

And he said, Thou speakest in Riddles.

And I said. There are two processions that never stop, and they go in opposite ways, and I ride in them both. And I jump constantly from one to the other. For I ride behind the Hearse and have no time to change my clothes or my mind before I ride to the Wedding. And the sounds of the Dirge mingle ever in mine ears with those of the Wedding March. And the rattling of the rice on the windows of the carriage is echoed by the sound of the dust falling upon the coffin in the grave.

And he said, I cannot understand how a man can stand it. I should think it would drive thee crazy. But perchance it cometh not so hard when a man getteth used to it?

And I said, Friend, I never shall get used to it. There lieth some part of my heart in every grave where I have stood and committed dust to dust. The joy of the bride and the hope of the bridegroom are as mine own joy and hope.

And he said. Thine must be a sadly mixed life. I envy thee not thy job. Yea, I have thought mine own job a hard one, but thou canst give me cards and spades.

And I said, O my friend, there again thou art mistaken. For my work is one of joy. When I go unto the house of mourning, there do I go with a message of comfort and hope. And when I meet the bride and the groom before the Altar of God and bless them ere they go forth to the establishment of a new home, then do I add to their joy. And when they come again and meet me there and bring with them a little child, of whose like is the Kingdom of God, then again is their joy the more perfect by reason of that which I say and do in the name of the Lord.

And he said, Nevertheless, I shall remember hereafter that the business of being a prophet of the Lord calleth for more agility than I had supposed.

And I said, There may be no harm in that.

Perhaps

I spake unto Keturah, saying, I must hie me unto the shop of the Barber.

Now the daughter of the daughter of Keturah was there, and she spake unto me, saying, Grandpa, the Barber giveth unto every one that hath his hair cut a Stick of Gum. Wilt thou bring the Gum unto me?

And I answered and said unto her, Alas, my little maiden, it cannot be. Youth hath many privileges which belong not unto those advanced in years, and among them is the privilege of receiving Gum from the Barber. If there come unto the shop of the Barber a nice little girl, and she sitteth very quietly in his chair while he bobbeth her hair just below her ears, unto her doth he give a Stick of Gum. And peradventure there come unto his shop a Small Boy, and he maketh no fuss, but remaineth quietly in the chair, and goeth forth smiling ke Mr. Zip-zip-zip, with his hair cut just as short as mine, unto him also doth the Barber give a Stick of Gum. But unto aged men like unto thy Grandpa doth he give no Gum, yea, though they be never so good. Rejoice in thy youth, and congratulate thyself that thou hast entered into the Kingdom of Heaven as a little child. For youth there is balm in Gilead, but for Grandpa there is no Gum in Goodness.

And she said, Grandpa, across the street from the shop of the Barber is a Drug Store. And in the Drug Store there is Gum. Howbeit, they give thee not one stick but five, and thou shalt give unto the man in the white coat a Nickel.

And I said, Between one stick which the Barber giveth free and five sticks which the man with the white coat in the Drug Store giveth for a nickel, is a measurable difference in good hard Cash.

And she waited a moment, and she said, Grandpa, wilt thou bring me the Gum?

And I said. Perhaps.

And she considered, and she asked, saying, Grandpa, what is the meaning of "Perhaps"?

And I said, the word Perhaps is a word of widely different connotations. For sometimes it meaneth, Not if I can think of some good reason for not doing it. And again it meaneth, It shall never be done. And once, a very long time ago, when I asked something of thy Grandma, and she said, Perhaps, that was a meaning still different.

And she said, Grandpa, what doth Perhaps mean when a little girl asketh her Grandpa for Gum and she asketh him very nicely and sayeth Please?

And I said. It meaneth that she shall have the Gum.

And she got it.

Now Keturah heard all this, and she said nothing, but I saw her smiling as though the little maiden were learning some things which her grandmother knew a long time ago.

And I said unto Keturah, I wonder if I could write a Parable about the different meanings of a word?

And Keturah said, Perhaps.

The Courage of the Captain

It came to pass many years ago, that I journeyed, and I rode upon a Steamboat upon the Great River, even the Mississippi. And there occurred a fight upon the lower deck of the boat, and one man stabbed another man in the neck, so that he bled much. And he would have stabbed him again and killed him, save that the Captain descended from the Hurricane Deck, and whether he descended by the Stairs or by a Parachute, or whether he Leaped Down, no one could remember. And the Captain came between the men as they fought, and took away the knife from the man who had it, and brought it unto me with the blood still wet upon it, and said, Here is a Pretty Little Souvenir of life upon the River.

And I have that knife unto this day.

Now on that boat they told me much about the Captain, how that he feared God, but neither man nor devil; and how that he was Boss of the Boat from the Boiler Room to the Pilot House, and that no man dared bat an eye until he first had permission from the Old Man. For upon the Mississippi the name of the Captain of all boats is the Old Man.

And the Captain took me into his own room hard by the Pilot House, and behold, it was a Young Arsenal. For he had a Magazine Rifle, and a Pair of Revolvers, and some more Revolvers, and a Knife. And men spake softly when they passed that room, for few of them had seen the inside of it, and they had heard terrible things about the number of men whom the Captain had slaughtered and eaten before breakfast when they Got Gay on his boat.

But all men held the Old Man in honor, neither was there a man on the boat but would have fought for him, save that the Old Man bade every man stand back and not get hurt while he attended to matters.

And when the Captain fought, he carried with him no Gun nor Knife nor Stick, but his Bare Hands only. And in his room were Dirks and Guns and Brass Knuckles that he had taken away from men who fought.

Now after many years I met the Captain, and he had retired from the River. And we sat and talked long together.

And I said, I have seen many brave men, but I incline to the Opinion that thou art a Little Bit the bravest piece of sheer manhood I have ever known.

And the Captain said, Deceive not thyself. I am a man of Great Timidity. Therefore did I always make it a point to get into the Fight Right Away; and when I got in, then, of course, even a coward doth know that he must see it through. But had I waited to consider, then should I never have fought; for I am Very Timid. But it was my Duty to keep Order on my Boat, and when I dealt with Gamblers and Cutthroats and with drunken Roustabouts, then did I know exactly what I was Up Against, and acted accordingly.

And I asked him. How many men hast thou killed and eaten?

And he said. It is my daily comfort and for it I devoutly thank my God, that I never inflicted any permanent injury on any fellow man.

And I said, How often didst thou get hurt?

And he said, I was on the River from the time I was eight years old until I was three score and ten, and I never got a scratch.

And I said, I still think thee a most brave man.

But he answered, Nay, it was lucky for me that men knew not how much of a Coward I was, and that I never had time to think. For being a Timid Man, I got into the fight at the start.

And I said. Blessed are the peacemakers who get into the fight at the start, and save lives and do brave deeds and keep the boat in order and neither hurt nor get hurt.

And he said. It may be so. But I was always a Timid Man.

But I still think him the Bravest Man I have known.

Rising Above the Clouds

I rode upon a Railway Train; and we were in the Rocky Mountains. And we awoke in the morning, and the Train was climbing, with two Engines pulling us, and one pushing behind. And we were nigh unto Twelve Furlongs above the Sea.

And it came to pass as we ascended, that there were clouds below us, and Clouds upon the sides of Mountains, but there were no Clouds above us, but the clear shining of the Morning Sun.

And there came unto me a small Girl and her younger Brother, who were riding upon the Train, and we talked about the Clouds. For so did John Ruskin, and Aristophanes, and the little lad was very happy, and he said,

I have never been above the Clouds before.

And his sister was Worldly-wise. And she said, A Cloud ain't nothing but just fog.

And he said, Nay, but this is more. And behold now, how then is a Cloud just under us, and we ride upon the top of it?

And she said. We are on the Rails, just as we always have been; and there can't nobody ride on a Cloud.

And the boy said, Jesus can ride upon a Cloud; for I saw a Picture of Him.

And the little girl said. Yes, but that ain't us.

Now the little girl may have been right; but I thought within myself that this world hath too many people who look out on Life through her windows. For they see no sunlit Clouds, but only Fog; and they have little faith in rising above Clouds, but have confidence only in the Rails.

And I do not despise Rails, nor advise people to discard them and ride upon Clouds. Nevertheless, I have seen people rise above Clouds, and live in the sunlight of God. And I have known others who, whenever it is said unto them,

Thus have other men done, or thus did the good Lord Jesus, make reply. Yes, but that ain't us.

And if it is spoken concerning the House of God, Thus did the Synagogue in Jonesville, and thus was it done by the Church in Smithville, they answer. Yes, but that ain't us.

And if it be said, Thou shouldest be a better man; for other men have risen above thy Clouds and thine Infirmities, they say. Yes, but that ain't us.

And when it is said, Thus hath the grace of God abounded in other lives, they say. Yes, but that ain't us.

But if it ain't, why ain't it?

For this cause did God dwell in human flesh that men should never count any good thing impossible that they behold in the dear Lord Jesus.

For he is our peace, who hath broken down all middle walls, that men should no longer say, But that ain't us.

The Oyster Shell

I have a friend who hath a Summer Cottage by the Seaside. And he said unto me, Come and spend a day with me and I will give thee the

Time of thy Sweet Young Life. And I spent the day, and he did all that he said he would do, and among the things that he did to me was a Shore Dinner. And we ate Clam Chowder and Fried Mackerel, and Stewed Cod and Baked Bluefish, and Lobster Salad. Likewise did we eat Stewed Clams and Oysters on the Half Shell. And I gave thanks to God who made me to suck of the Abundance of the Seas and of treasures hid in the Sands.

Now while we were eating the Oysters I was thinking, and I said. He was a Brave Man who ate the first Oyster. And as I spake I bit upon something hard. And behold it was a pearl, albeit not a very good one.

And we spake of the Pearl, and how it cometh of an Hurt to the Oyster, that is made by a Grain of Sand, that getteth into the Shell, and the Oyster cannot get it out; and how it Woundeth him sore, so that there cometh from the Oyster a very Precious juice that congealeth where the Sand doth irritate, and maketh a pearl.

And my friend saith, It is a pity that Pearl thou hast found is not a good one; for then couldest thou have sold it and gotten thee gain.

And I answered, Though I sell it not, yet have I gotten gain therefrom.

And he said, Tell me how.

And I said, The oyster is not in all respects the highest type of a Christian; yet in this hath he something to teach even to Christian men, so that there is no man but may learn from him and be wiser.

And he said, It may be so, but all this is news to me.

And I said, Oh, my friend, the race of mankind liveth. Each man in his own Oyster Shell, and no man knoweth fully what hurt another man hideth. But there is no shell that shutteth out the irritating Sands of Grief and Circumstance, and few men meet the cutting, wounding intrusions of life so well as doth the Oyster. I have been young and am now old, and I have seen men in all manner of misfortune, and have seen them meet life's adversities in every possible manner. There may not be much that a Christian can learn from an Oyster, but the Good God so made the world as that even the Oyster may speak to men who now are crushed by their sorrows and say to them, Heal thy hurt with a Pearl.

The Gravity Trolley

I journeyed unto a distant State, even to California, and I rode upon a Trolley that ran Six Miles back from the Railway Station into the hills. And I observed that all the way as we Ascended, the Motorman consumed Electric Current, but when we Descended, then did he shut off the Juice, and controlled our speed by means of the Brake, with an Emergency Brake at hand, and I spake unto certain of those with whom I rode, of the Trolley, and of how the Road-bed was all Up-Hill one way, and all Down-Hill the other way; and how they used two different kinds of Power, even Electricity and Gravitation, and each of them in one direction only.

And one of them spake unto me, saying. Thus it was intended when this Road was Surveyed, and before they had Electric Power; for in that day did they haul the cars Up-Hill with Mules; and there was a Platform upon the Rear of the Car, and the Mules Ascended the Platform and rode down. And they told me how the Mules soon learned the trick, so that as soon as they were unhitched they hastened to the rear of the car and climbed up.

And others told me many things about those Mules; and a certain Woman procured for me a Picture of the Car with the Passengers riding Inside and the Mules riding Outside, and the Mules enjoying it as much as the Passengers. And it pleased me much.

Now it came to pass in time that the Electric Current Emancipated the Mules, and the Owners of the Trolley sold the Mules. And farmers bought them at a good price, for the Mules were fat and strong. But it was a Bad Buy for the farmers.

For those Mules would pull the Plow Up-Hill to the end of the Furrow, and then turn around and seek to climb up on the rear end of the Plow in order that they might ride down! And when they found no Platform, then were they Troubled in their Mind and much Bewildered. Neither was it Possible ever to teach them to pull any load Down-Hill.

Now I know many people with whom this System worketh the other way, and who are very willing to be hitched up to a job that runneth down hill by Gravity or the labor of others, but who insist upon riding or being Unhitched when the Trolley hitteth the up-grade. For the work of the Lord hath its Up-Hill and its Down-Hill aspects, and if there be any Platforms provided for those who would ride, thou shalt find them already occupied by kindred souls who have beaten them to it.

The Frog and the Hornet

There came to me a man who said,
I have many unpleasant experiences.
And I said unto him, Thou art not the Only Pebble on the Beach.

And he said, But mine are such as I cannot speak of, and they Humiliate me. For my occupation is such that I am beholden to those who Exasperate me, yet must I say nothing, and it is not easy to Grin and Bear it.

And I said unto him, I walked one day through the Forest, and I came upon a Little Pool. And in the margin of the Pool was there a Frog. And he sat as Immovable as the Sphinx sitteth amid the sands; so sat he in the mud.

And as I regarded him, there came an Hornet, and lighted a little space away from him, as it were an half or two parts of a Cubit. And the Frog gave no sign that he saw the Hornet or me, but sat in the mud immovable. But when the Hornet let down his wings and began to sip of the water that was in the mud, then did the Frog leap. And it was a marvelous leap, for he seemed to make No Preparation for it, neither to pull himself together or to take thought of the distance, but rose as if he had been shot from a Gun, and landed so that his mouth came exactly where the Hornet was. And the Frog Gobbled the Hornet before the Hornet realized that Anything Had Occurred.

Now when I saw that, I said. That was a Mighty Good Jump, and accurately measured, but that Frog hath procured for himself a Prize Package the nature whereof he knoweth not. And I looked that the Hornet should have bored him full of Gimlet Holes from the inside out. And I said. Surely that Frog will immediately display all the Characteristic Symptoms of Appendicitis.

But if it gave him Stomach Ache he showed it not, but settled himself in the same old place, and waited as if he were the more content for having had a pinch of Mustard with his Meat.

And I said unto the man. Be like unto that Frog. And if thou must swallow a Sting with thy Daily Bread, do it so Contentedly that no man shall know that thou hast colic. But if the time cometh to leap, then do thou leap so that thou shalt swallow not only the Sting but the Stinger.

And he said. Shall I wait till I may avenge myself?

And I said, There are more kinds of revenge than one. And most of them hurt the Avenger more than the Avenged; so that I commend them not. Consider the Divers Kinds, and be ready for that which is best, and if thou forget all thought of revenge, so much the better. Meantime, let not the sting interfere with thy Digestion nor thy Prayer.

The Barometer

There was a day when I went down to the Sea in Ships, and made a Voyage on Great Waters. And when I returned to my Home, I brought a Barometer, which Sailors call a Glass. And Keturah esteemeth it not, and declareth that it telleth what the Weather was Yesterday. But I think Highly of it.

Now there came to me a man who had been a Sinner, and he had Repented. But at times his Temptations beset him so that he Fell. And he wept much as he told me of his sins.

And I said. How often didst thou Get Drunk in the old days?

And he answered. Just once, and it Lasted Over Continually.

And I said. When thou didst first repent, how frequently didst thou fall?

And he said, About once in a Month.

And I said, How long is it now Between Falls?

And he said. Sometimes Three Months, and Sometimes Six. I gain a Little, but it is Very Slow. And the longer it is between Falls, the more I Despise Myself that I should fall at all.

And I asked him, What dost thou think of the Weather?

And he was astonished at my question, but he answered, and said. It is a Rainy Day.

And I said. This is a fine Barometer. What doth it say?

And he saith, The Finger pointeth to Rain.

And I tapped lightly on the Glass and the finger moved upward a Very Little.

And I said. Before tomorrow Night it will be Fair.

And he said, How can that be when the Barometer saith Rain?

And I said. There was an old Sailor man who swore to me by the gods of the sea, even Neptune and Davy Jones, saying, A Barometer is an Everlasting Liar if thou readest only the words around the Dial. For it is Not a Question of Where it Pointeth only, but Which Way it Moveth.

And I said, My friend, thy Soul's Barometer Moveth Upward. Trust God, keep up thy Courage and thou shalt Surely Conquer.

And as he went his way, Lo, the clouds parted, and there appeared a Little Patch of Blue Sky.

The Private Car

There is a certain man whose abiding place is a city where is a great Railway Station, even a Terminal, and this man determined within himself that he would go upon a Journey. So he walked unto the Terminal, and he bought a Ticket, and he paid the Fare. And he presented the Ticket at a Gate where stood a Watchman and the Watchman punched his Ticket and spake unto him saying. Thy train is all ready on Track Number Six.

And he beheld the Cars, and they were filling up rapidly. And he said, Behold, they will all be crowded, and I shall suffer Discomfort.

And he beheld the last Car, which was nearest unto the Gate, and behold, there was no one in it. And he said,

This will I do. I will go into that Car, and I shall have Abundant Room.

So he went within, and he had all the Room he Wanted, even the Whole Car. And he smiled within himself when he thought of the other Passengers who were Jammed into the other Cars.

And while he was Hugging Himself for Joy, and considering what a smart Guy he was, behold, the train pulled out, and left him and his Private Car standing upon the track.

And he rushed out and spake angrily unto the Watchman, and he said. Wherefore am I left behind?

And the Watchman said, That is an Extra Car which we keep on the track to use in case there be a greater crowd than we expect, but today there was no great crowd. Yea, and there had been room enough for thee in one of the cars that went, but thou didst want more room, and thou hast all the room in sight. Yea, and upon the Side Track out in the yard are many empty cars. Thou canst take thy seat in any one of them. But if thou desirest to ride unto the City for which thy Ticket readeth, behold there will be another train in four hours and fifteen minutes; and take heed that thou enter the cars that go.

Now, this I beheld, for I was in the Station, even the Terminal, and I saw that man, yea, and I heard that man: and what I heard was a plenty.

And I considered that often I am caught in the Jam of life, with people crowding and pushing, and it were much more comfortable to find a quiet seat in some Rear Car, where the wicked cease from troubling and the weary are at rest. But I considered how that if a man is to get anywhere he must go with Folks, even though they crowd, and that no one man can do very much without the companionship and help of other men. Therefore did I resolve to keep out of the Private Cars that do not go nor get a man anywhere but learn the art of going and working with other men. For I have seen that for the lack of the ability to do this, some men are left on the track in their own Private Car, while the enterprises of life move on.

Reformers

There came unto me a Reformer, and desired me to join his Organization for the Elimination of Superfluous Buttons from the Back of the Coats of Men. And he solicited my Contribution. And he did not persuade me to part with any of my Hard Earned Cash. And he read unto me Statisticks concerning the number of men who had been Held Up by Robbers catching hold of the Buttons as they were fleeing, and of the men who were caught in Machinery and pulled in by the Buttons. And he had computed that if the cost of the Buttons were saved, it would provide Chewing gum and Nose powder for Nine Million Stenographers for a Thousand Years.

And I said, There are More Important Evils for me to fight.

And he said, How darest thou say that any Evil is unimportant?

And I said, I know not what Evils God esteemeth small, or whether He esteemeth any Evil to be Unimportant. But I know that no one man can fight all the evils in the world at one time, save within his own soul; and that the officer who marcheth his men against Impregnable Breastworks is Court Martialed and Shot; and he who fireth a Big Bertha to kill a Mosquito is cashiered. Therefore will I fight the evils which I can probably overcome, and which are great enough to deserve my Limited Effort.

And he said. Thou art an Apologist for Sin.

And I said. Thou liest. Nevertheless, hear a Parable. There is a certain City where the Police went on strike. And that was not so Appalling as the fact that Thousands of men who had appeared Lawful broke out forthwith in Lawlessness. And after certain days of Window-smashing and Looting and Violence, when Order began to be restored, there came unto the Chief Captain of the Police a Committee of certain good men who said, Behold, there are a Thousand Games of Craps running Wide-open on the Common, and only Six Policemen, and they heed it not. Now send more Policemen, and stop them.

And the Chief Captain called his Sergeant, and he said. Pull off them Six Cops, and send them to Scollay Square; and see if thou canst start a few Crapgames in Harvard Yard or around Bunker Hill Monument.

And he said unto the Committee, Those Thousand Crap Games look Awful Good to me. They mean that there are about Four Thousand men there who might otherwise be Raising Rough House in Scollay Square; and they are taking the Long Green from one another instead of Sticking-up law-abiding citizens. Unto every man whom I find Shooting Craps will I give Absent Treatment.

And the Reformer said, Evil is always Evil and should always be opposed.

And I said, The Crap-shooting on the Common was a Temporary Mustard Plaster to draw Congestion from Inflamed Spots.

And the Reformer said, I verily believe that thou art thyself a wearer of Buttons upon the Back of thy Coat. Turn thee around that I may see and rebuke thee.

And I said, Thou shalt not see my back, but I will Mighty Soon see thine.

And I opened the Front Door and he departed.

And this I did, not that I would call any Evil Small, but that even good men and Reformers are entitled to a moderate sense of proportion.

The Man Who Saw New York

A certain man went to New York, and he bought him an Excess Fare Ticket, and he boarded the Twentieth Century Limited, and he felt very important because he was getting off one portion of the surface of the earth and upon another somewhat more swiftly than did his grandfather when he traversed the same road in the other direction three score years and ten before. For his grandfather drave an ox-cart westward and saved money, and he drave the Twentieth Century eastward and flung money out of the car window. And in that fashion do men of this generation rise to a position of superiority above their grandfathers.

And he came into the city of Little Old New York. And he entered a great Inn hard by the station, so that he entered it by the Subway, and he went not upon the street.

And when the morning came he entered the Subway again, and ran down to Wall Street. And the building where he did business had its own Subway Entrance, so that his feet pressed not the soil of New York.

And he descended again into the Subway and returned unto Forty-second Street, for he had an errand in Times Square, and he followed the Green Line to the Shuttle Train, and did his business in Times Square, and he followed the Black Line back to the Shuttle Train and he returned unto Forty-second Street. And a friend invited him to lunch at the Yale Club, and he entered that from the Subway. And he took an Uptown Express and went many miles, and he poked his head out of the Subway long enough to see Grant's Tomb. Then he looked at his watch and hastened back into the Subway and returned to the Inn, and paid his bill, which was Some Bill, and he grabbed his bag and hustled into the Subway and followed the Green Line to the Shuttle Train, and got off at Times Square and took the Downtown Express to the Pennsylvania Station and entered it from the Subway, and returned unto his home.

And he said unto his friends, I have seen Little Old New York; and behold, it is an Hole in the Ground.

But New York hath an Elevated as well as a Subway, and he knew it not. And it hath cars that travel on the surface as well as those that go above and below it; and busses that go up Fifth Avenue, and Rubberneck wagons with a man with a megaphone. And it hath Churches and Libraries and Art Galleries, and he had seen only the Subway.

And many a man goeth into a strange city and hunteth out its underground life, and saith, It is a wicked, wicked city. But the city was not wicked save only that wicked men acted wickedly in it.

And, beloved, there be those who travel through life in the Subway: neither do they even suspect how large is God's world above ground, nor how nobly a man may live who keepeth himself upon an higher level.

And I considered these things, and I said in mine heart that I will live the life of one who useth this world at its best, and who discovereth in it more than that which may be discovered by the life of the Subway.

The Cocoanut Cakes

I was not always aged, but was once young. And I sojourned in a School of the Prophets. And on the day before the Sabbath I rode every week Nineteen Miles that on the Sabbath Day I might speak the word of God to the people in a Little White Synagogue with a Tall Steeple. And on the day after the Sabbath I rode back again. And there were times when the Roads were bad, so that for every foot that my horse went forward, he sank in the mud unto the depth of an half of a foot; so I went down through Nine Miles and the half of a Mile of mud before I got there. But when I arrived then did the good people welcome me into warm homes and clean beds and set before me hot suppers.

For I boarded around among them.

And at the first place where I abode for a Sabbath, the good woman set before me Cocoanut Cake. And I ate plentifully thereof.

Now the women of the other homes inquired of her, saying. How didst thou like the Young Minister? And is he hard to entertain? And doth he cause thee much trouble? And is he fussy? And what doth he like to eat?

And she said. He is not fussy, and he keepeth out of the kitchen, and when he hath a book he doth not bother the hostess with Theology; and he said unto me that Cocoanut Cake is his Favorite Cake.

Now all the women told all the other women, saying, The Young Minister loveth Cocoanut Cake.

And they all knew how to make Cocoanut Cake, and they all made it. And wherever I went, there did they set before me Cocoanut Cake.

Now thou wilt surely think within thine heart that I got so much Cocoanut Cake that I abhorred it, and that I have never liked it since. But thou hast another Think coming. For thou knowest not what sort of Cocoanut Cake the women of that Parish make. Yea, for three years did I eat it with scarce ever a break in the record, save that there also they make Cake with Maple Sugar Frosting. And he that hath eaten that kind of Cake knoweth that that is about the best ever.

For there be some things of which no man can ever have too much. And when mine heart goeth back across the years, then do I remember the long rides, and the times that I drave up in the dark and the cold, and how they stabled mine horse knee-deep in clean straw, and put a sack of oats under the buggy-seat when I departed, and maybe also a Bushel of Potatoes or a Sack of Apples or a Can of Maple Syrup. And I know that I shall never have too much of any of the good things which they bestowed upon me, nor of the love that was in them all.

And now and then as the years go by, and one and another of those I loved is called unto his long home, then do they send for me to come and say a word of love before the dust returneth unto dust. And ever there is some good woman who hath a table set for me in her home; and there do I always find Cocoanut Cake.

And whenever I eat of Cocoanut Cake that is Unusually Nice, then do I remember the friends of my early Ministry as a Messenger of God, and I love them yet.

The Viol That Was Almost in Tune

Whether a man that is Regenerate hath all parts of him equally Regenerate, hath been discussed by grave men in councils of old time. And I have sometimes inquired of my soul whether there lingered in me any element of the unregenerate that had gotten as far down as my Toes. And this question I ask myself when I listen to Musick other than that of the Sanctuary, even to the Viol, which the profane call the Fiddle, when it is Played Skillfully. For when it playeth of an Ancient man named Daniel whose surname was Tucker, or discourseth upon the wonders of creation in Pop goeth the Weasel, or relateth the adventures of the Pilgrim in Arkansaw, then do I notice that my Sandals rise a little space from the Floor and come down again.

Now I was in the home of a friend whose Daughter had taken lessons upon the Viol, and she essayed to play for me. And she sawed long upon her Instrument to get it worse out of tune than it was already, and she said, I have not a very Good ear for the Tuning, but I can play the melody well.

And she played me a Polonaise in A Flat. And the Polonaise I comprehended not, but the A Flat I was fully conscious of. And I noticed that she had the Technique Down Fine. For she first folded a Silk Handerchief and placed it against her Neck where the Viol Rested, and the Handkerchief was well chosen for the Harmony of its Color with her Dress, and needed it at that place. Likewise did she Vibrate her finger upon the String as her teacher had Instructed her. And she drew her Bow with the precision of a Director of Calisthenics.

But her A string was Flat, and her E string was Sharp, and her other strings were both of them Just a Little Bit Off.

And her father listened with Pride, for he had paid Three Hundred Dollars for the Instrument, and more than that for the Teacher, and his daughter had learned to Render Great Compositions, even Polonaises in A Flat and such like Music, and she had acquired Technique, and the proper method of folding her Silk Handkerchief. But she had not the Kingdom of God within her so that she should know when all four of her Strings were a Little Bit off.

Now I would rather that my daughter and my sons should play for me Musick which is Less Ambitious, and play it upon Well Tuned Instruments, even the Money Musk, and the Irish Washerwoman and the Turkey in the Straw, than to render for my Edification Polonaises in A Flat wherein I get more of the Flatness than of the Polonaise.

For a Simple thing that is rendered Artistically is effective when an Ambitious thing poorly done is the more conspicuously a Failure. And there be many things well played as to technique whereof the strings are a Little Bit Off.

The Roadrunner

I and Keturah we went unto a far land, even unto California, and we sojourned there certain days. And our friends in that place were kind unto us, neither did we set foot upon the ground if they could prevent it; for they took us in their gas-driven Chariots, and showed unto us a Good Time.

And as we rode along a great Highway, we beheld a Bird, that is tall and graceful, that runneth along the road or beside it, and that seldom flieth. And they called that Bird the Roadrunner.

And they told me this story about that Bird, and I know not if it be true or false; save that I think no one in California would speak falsely about anything, save it might be to indulge in a Very Mild Exaggeration concerning the Climate. And this is the story which they told unto me:

The Roadrunner hath an inveterate enemy in the Rattlesnake; and he avoideth not the Snake by flying, as do other birds, but he runneth along the ground, where the Snake doth sometimes get him. Now a Rattlesnake enjoyeth a good sound sleep upon the sunny top of a Rock, or in some other warm place. And when a Roadrunner seeth a Rattlesnake asleep, he hasteneth and calleth all the other Roadrunners. And they come, and every one beareth in his beak a pad which he plucketh from the Cactus that groweth where the Snakes and the Roadrunners most do congregate. And they draw nigh quietly, and lay their Cactus Ringwise round the Serpent. Then do they go away and get Some More Cactus. And when they have laid that, then do they go away again, and Get Some More, and Then Some. And the Serpent sleepeth and heareth them not.

And when they have him Walled In, then do they waken him. And he rouseth himself from his slumbers, and behold, there is a Roadrunner nigh unto him. And he coileth himself and striketh at the Roadrunner, but pricketh himself upon the Cactus. Then doth a Roadrunner approach him fiom the other side, and he doeth likewise. And it cometh to pass in time that the Serpent becometh Crazy, and striketh at random, and every time he woundeth himself in a new place. And when the Roadrunners see that he hath gone Clean Nutty, then do they leap over him, and draw nigh unto him, and even pick at him with their bills; and when he striketh back, behold he landeth every time against the Cactus Thorns. Thus doth he Sting Himself To Death, and the Roadrunners hold a Merry Wake above him.

Now I have seen men who were Hemmed In after this fashion, so that what a certain poet hath called the Fell Clutch of Circumstance doth hold them in its grip, and Tantalize them so that they Sting Themselves to Death in their Frantick Efforts to break through. And mine heart grieveth for them.

And unto every one of them would I speak, saying. Oh, my brother, I know not how to break a way for thee through the Thorny Hedge that doth encompass thee; but this I know, it is not Good Sense nor yet Religion that thou shouldest Impale Thyself upon the Thorns. Whatever thou doest, go not Daffy over it, for then shalt thou work thine own destruction. Consider first of all, that there is one direction where the path is not closed, and that is Up. Calm thine own spirit, and look unto God; so shalt thou face with whatever good sense thou hast, and it is not much, and whatever grace a Mighty God can give unto thee, and that may be Considerable, the situation which thou art Up Against. And fret not thyself because of the Roadrunners. Keep thou still, and let them do the Worrying. And if thou lose not the little Sense thou hast, and employ the abundant grace which God shall give unto thee, there will yet appear somewhere a little Crevice among the Cactus; and albeit thou be Pricked in getting out, still it will not kill thee. And thou shalt yet outlive the Roadrunners.

Wherefore, possess thy soul in patience; trust in thy God, and when thou findest a Hole in the Cactus, though it prick thee, Go To It, and Go Through.

The Guest-Room Towels

There came to me a man who said. The trouble with thee, and with the Church, and with all who labor with thee, is that thy Methods are Old. We are living in a New Age, and the Old Methods are Inadequate.

And I answered. Thou speakest truly, and perhaps wisely.

And he said. How is it that if what I say is Certainly True it is only Possibly Wise?

And I answered him. Because there are no kinds of unwisdom so great as those that are founded on Truth that is Ill Considered. What New Methods dost thou advocate?

And he Got Busy with a Line of Talk about his New Methods, that never had been tried anywhere, and which were certain of but one thing, that they never would work.

And he said, How dost thou like my New Methods?

And I said unto him,

I went to a certain city, and lodged with a friend who sent me to my bed in the Guest Chamber. And it was a Comfortable Chamber, and his wife had made it ready for my coming. And among the other Preparations, she had hung the towel-rack full of New Linen Towels, which she had purchased by the Dozen, and there were Six of them in my Room. And they were Very Nice Towels, and well worth the Price that she paid, for Linen was Going Up. But when I essayed to wipe my face upon them, than I could not do it. For those Towels were every one of them as Stiff and as Shiny as a Sheet of Tin, and likewise as Impervious to Water. So I mussed them up, one of them and yet another and another till I had polished my face with the Metallic Surface of all six of them.

And I said unto him. There must needs be New Methods, and I would not be last in the use of any of them that are good. Neither do I care to be the first to dry my face upon a New Towel. Let him that is ambitious for New Experiments try it before me, and after it hath gone to the Laundry and come back, less Shiny but more Serviceable, then will I try it. It is enough for me that I must wear my own New Boots.

The Pens

I have a friend who is a maker of Gold Pens. And he said unto me, What dost thou know about Pens?

And I said, I live hard by a Pen, though not in one; for I am a Writer.

And he said. Come with me, and I will show thee how a Pen is made.

So we entered the Factory, and came into a room where was a Crucible. And a man took Fine Gold and weighed it and cast it into the Crucible; and Copper took he also. And out of the Crucible came forth an Ingot.

And another man took the Ingot and weighed it, and rolled it into a Sheet. And another man took the Sheet and weighed it, and cut it into Strips. And another man took the Strips and weighed them, and out of every one of them cut he Pens an hundred and forty and four.

And another man took the Pens and curved the sides thereof. And another man cut out of every several Pen an Hole that was shaped like an heart. And another man cut in every Pen a Slit.

And every man counted the Pens that were given him, insomuch that if one Pen had been lost, or so much as a grain of gold missing, it would have been known who had taken it.

Then did certain damsels take the Pens, and they burnished them and polished them, so that every Pen received of the labor of an hundred men and two score maidens.

And the garments that they wore are burned once in the space of three months, and from the ashes they save more than enough gold to buy new garments. And when they wash their hands the water runneth into a great Vat and settleth, so that in every month they take from the bottom of the vat gold to the value of three hundred shekels.

Now I had watched the making of one Pen from the time it came forth in the Ingot till it was completed. And my friend took that Pen, and caused it to be set in an holder, and gave it to me. And he said. Keep it, for it is thine.

And I bowed low and thanked him.

And he filled the holder with ink.

And I spake unto him, and said, Behold, thou hast showed me a wonderful thing, and I have learned much. But I will show thee a thing yet more wonderful. For I am filling this Pen not with ink only, but with memory and creative power. I will cause this Pen to tell the story of its own creation, so that men who live a thousand miles away shall see what I have seen this day.

And he said, Thine is the more wonderful art: for the making of a Pen is not so wonderful as the use thereof.

So I took the Pen, and I wrote this parable therewith. And I remembered the gold that did not become Pens, but became dust of gold in the garments, and that flowed down the pipe into the Vat. And I prayed to my God, and said, O my God, who willeth not that any of the children of men should perish, if the washings of men's hands yield not filth only but gold to the value of three hundred shekels in a month, what canst thou do with the souls of men, in the day when hearts are tried as gold is tried in the furnace?

And I know not the answer to my prayer, but my hope is in God.

Consistency

There came to me a man who said, Safed, thou speakest many wise words, but thou art not always consistent.

And I said unto him, If I were always consistent, then should I never be wise.

And he said. Thou utterest dark sayings.

Then said I unto him. There are no completely consistent men aside from those in the Cradle and in the Asylum for Imbeciles. The only consistent man is the Completely Ignorant Man. There once lived a Philosopher named Immanuel, whose surname was Kant, who showed unto men that any line of thought consistently followed doth bump up against the Impossible. Man doth begin life in complete Consistency, which is to say, that he beginneth it in complete Ignorance. But there cometh a day when he learneth a Truth, namely, that his Toe is capable of being brought up into his Mouth; and that Truth maketh his Ignorance Lopsided.

And he said unto me, I had not thought of that; but it cometh to pass in time that he can no longer get his Toe into his Mouth.

And I answered. So happeneth it with much of what we apprehend as Truth; by the time we learn it, the thing is no longer possible nor yet desirable; nevertheless, the Truth hath been worth the learning, and it hath its logical relation to other Inconsistencies, which are properly apprehended as Truth.

And he said unto me. Say on.

And I said, The circumference of men's Ignorance is vast, and every new Truth discovered is the Lengthened Radius whereby to measure the Diameter and Area of a Vaster Ignorance and a Greater Inconsistency. Yet hath it a Value. For each new Truth becometh an Interrogation Point, which reacheth out like a Fish Hook after the mouth of Leviathan. And albeit neither thou nor Job the servant of God can draw him out, yet doth the Interrogation Point Hook now and then a Sculpin of Information or an Hornpout of Knowledge, or some slippery Eel of Truth, which maketh our Ignorance Lopsided.

Furthermore, I said unto him, Men do walk, not by any process of Bisymmetrical Progressive Motion, but by Hitching one side Ahead, and then Pulling the other side up and a Little Ahead, and by throwing the Center of Gravity out of Plumb and catching themselves before they fall, so that in falling forward but never striking, and wabbling ahead with first one foot and then the other, we contrive an approach to Consistency through Inconsistency. And the process of the Advancement of Human Knowledge, yea and of Human Goodness, is more or less Like Unto it.

And he said, I have learned enough for one day.

And I said. Go now and learn something on the other side of thine Ignorance that will help to balance up. For a False Balance is an Abomination unto the Lord, and the best thing about Inconsistency is that it doth challenge us to learn another Truth.

Profanity

They laid a water-pipe in the road at the place where I and Keturah go in Summer; and the soil was stubborn and rocky. And when the men came for to dig, I took a Spade and digged for a little time in the trench with them. Likewise did I with the Pick and the Crowbar.

And the men said. Thou canst do work such as we do save it be only in one thing. For if we strike more Rock than we expect, or if the water flow into our trench, or if perad venture it cave in so that we have to dig it out again, canst thou do thy part of the Swearing?

And I answered and said, I will do it all.

And they said, It is liable to be a Large Contract.

And I said, Even so, I will assume it. All the Swearing that this job requireth, leave it to me.

And when the ditch caved in, or the water stood in the trench so that they had to pump it out, or they struck rock and had to blast, then did they say one to another. Swear not: for that is Safed's job.

And thus it came to pass that no Swearing was necessary, but only Muscle and Pumps and some Dynamite.

Now I considered how many people there be who swear by the use of Profane words, or by the Slamming of Doors, or by Scolding, and I thought that it would be well if there might be appointed an Official Swearer for all such like occasions, and that he should consider the matter carefully before Swearing or Scolding and see if some other way would answer just as well. For if the digger strike rock, and must use Dynamite as well as swear, he might as well use Dynamite instead of Swearing. And if Kindness will do the work instead of Scolding, then is the Scolding wasted or maybe worse.

Therefore am I open to Employment wherever there is need, to take the responsibility of all the Swearing and all the Scolding that shall be required, and if it be left to me, there will not be much of either.

For one should neither Swear nor Scold if there be any other way to accomplish the result desired; nor unless it is sure that Swearing or Scolding will do good.

For there is a lot of wasted Swearing and Scolding: and to scold is to swear.

The Evil and Good of Gossip

Once upon a time there were Two Fools. And one of those Fools was a man and the other was a woman. And that is a Bad Combination.

And there came unto them one of their friends, and spake unto them, saying,

Behold, people are talking about you; and what they say is Unpleasant. Have a care, therefore, lest what they say become More Unpleasant.

And when the Two Fools heard this, they spake one to another, and said,

We should worry about what People Say. For we have done nothing amiss, and we shall do nothing amiss. And they who speak evil of us seek only the evil that is in their own hearts.

They are Idle Gossips. Let them talk. We will give them something to Talk About.

Then these Two Fools proceeded to give the Gossips something to Talk About. And they succeeded beyond their Fondest Hopes.

And the more people talked, the more Defiant these Two Fools became.

And when they had gotten themselves into a Pretty Bad Mess of Publick Scandal, then did the Woman Fool come unto Keturah, and the Man Fool came unto me.

And we had what might be called a Foursome.

And the Woman Fool wept much; and the Man Fool swore.

And I said unto them, Ye are Two Fools with less than a Single Thought; two Nuts, and both of you Cracked.

And they said. Behold, we have done no wrong. Let the evil be unto those who evil think.

And I said. Nay; the evil is also unto those who cause others to think evil.

And the man said. When a man knoweth that he hath done nothing wrong, then may he stand in his Conscious Rectitude and face the Lying, Foul-mouthed world.

And I said. Save thine eloquence. For a righteous cause a man may face the world, but not for the sake of indulging his own Folly.

And Keturah spake unto the Woman Fool, and said, My dear, this world is prone to judge that things mean what they seem to mean. Thou must not do the things that seem evil and expect the world to reckon it unto thee for good. If we are taught not to let our good be evil spoken of, much more must we not let our folly appear as if it had been evil.

And the Woman Fool said, I think that Gossip is the Vilest Thing in the World.

And I said, Gossip is indeed an unlovely thing. But it hath its Value to a Community.

And the man said. Thou speakest falsely. It hath no Value.

And I said, If it were not for the fear of Gossip, and the Wholesome Dread of what people would say, then would Fools such as ye are behave even worse than they now do; and that is a Plenty.

And I said. There are Fools that may be brayed in a Mortar with a Pestle and their folly will not depart from them. That Mortar is Public Sentiment, and that Pestle is Gossip. The braying is a Painful Process, but for you it may be Profitable.

Now it came to pass that those Two Fools were not quite Hopeless Fools. And they did as I and Keturah told them to do. And by this time their Folly is well-nigh forgotten.

The Kind of People in Our Town

There were two men who came newly into the City wherein I dwell. And it came to pass that they came both of them to visit me on the day of their arrival. For the one of them desired that he might borrow a Screwdriver: and the other besought me that he might use my Telephone to call up the Gas Company and the Electrick Light Company and the Butcher and the Baker and the Candlestick Maker.

And they inquired of me, both of them, saying. What Kind of People live in this Town, and of what Sort of Folk are my neighbors? And of each of them I asked, saying. What Kind of neighbors didst thou leave behind thee; and of what Sort were the Folk in the Old Home Town?

And the first of them answered and said. The Town I come from is an One Horse Town: and the Folk are a set of Four-Flushers; and they spend more money than they earn; and they are Unneighborly and Unpleasant; and they have so many Scandals that we kept ourselves apart like Lot in Sodom; because our righteous souls were vexed within us; and we shook off the dust of our feet and fled from that Burg and we looked not back.

And I said unto him, Thou wilt find this Town very much the same.

And while he yet Spake, the other came; and he asked of me the same question. And I likewise inquired of him concerning the Folk in his Old Home Town.

And he said,

They were fine Folk; and good neighbors; and it gave us pain to leave them; but Business called us here, and we had to leave our dear old friends.

And I said,

It is the same in this Town; and thou wilt find the People just as fine and good.

And the first man heard, and he was horrified; And he said.

Verily, thou art an old Liar; for thou didst tell me the folk of this Town were a Bunch of Grafters, and a Gang of Thugs.

And I said unto them both.

Listen unto me, and consider what I say. For I have told you both the truth. There are in Every Town two sorts of Folk. There are as many kinds of Folk in this town as there be in Oshkosh or Kalamazoo or Medicine Hat or Benares or Hong Kong. Thou canst find either sort.

But what I said is still more true; for each man is likely to find the town of the same sort as himself. May the Lord deliver me from having as a Neighbor a man who cometh from a Town of which he speaketh ill. For then should the word of the Prophet be fulfilled, saying,

And I will shew no mercy, saith the Lord,, but will deliver every man into the hand of his neighbor.

And I said unto them both,

If thou wouldest live in a good Town, be good thyself. So shall thine own Town be partly good, and thou shalt be the good in it, and help to make it better. It is a dirty bird that doth befoul its own nest, and a mighty poor Citizen who doth knock his own Town.

The Ethiopian Maiden and The Alarm Clock

Now in the Synagogue where I minister is there a good man with a Conscience like that of a Gadfly, and the Misdirected Zeal of a Flea, insomuch that he is always Stirring Things up.

And it is his wont to rise in the congregation when it is assembled for Prayer and for Waiting upon the Lord, with oftentimes more Waiting than Prayer, to say.

This Church should Rouse itself and waken to its Opportunity. We should be Active. We should not continually live at This Poor Dying Rate.

And all that he saith is Very True, and Very Irritating and Very Ineffective.

For those whom he thus addresseth are those of the Saving Remnant who already are aroused, or who have Slumbered in Prayer Meeting since the World Began, and can continue to ride in their Spiritual Pullman until it reacheth the Grand Terminal of Heaven, and they will never do any one any Harm.

But all the activity of this Good Brother is Geared to no Productive Machinery. It Cutteth No Ice.

Now there came a time when his Wordy Exhortation got upon my Nerve. And I spake unto him, saying, If thou desirest the Church to Rouse, then Rouse thou thyself, and be silent, but Saw Wood. For there were better things for thee to do than to Run thy Vocabulary in High Gear and never slip thy Clutch into anything that will make thine own wheels go around. For thou hast been right where thou art, in the middle of the Road, honking thy horn to others to Speed Up ever since I have known thee. Yea, and every little Christian in the Church doth get somewhere in his little Ford Car, save thou only. And thou occupiest Valuable Roadspace, and usest the whole power of thy Six Cylinder Lungs in Honking up other Christians who need it not.

And he was amazed, and he answered me nothing.

And I spake unto him this parable, saying,

Thou art like unto an Alarm Clock which Keturah bought, and presented it unto the Ethiopian Maiden who wrought in her Kitchen, that she might Rise and Cook the Breakfast while we slept. For that Alarm Clock did assuredly wake at an unearthly hour every morning every soul in the house save only the Ethiopian Maiden.

And after I had thus spoken, it was as long as Six Weeks before this Good Brother did again speak in the meeting for Prayer and for Waiting upon the Lord.

The Contented Conductor

The Conductor who took up my Ticket had upon his arm many Golden Stripes. And I said unto him, I perceive that thou hast been long upon the Road.

And he said. Forty and two years have I been a Passenger Conductor, and before that I ran a Freight, and before that I was a Brakeman.

And I said, Thou dost not look it.

And he said, If I still have Vigor for a man of mine age it is because I have learned two things. The first is to think first what is best and endeavor to attain it. The next is to be content with what I get. For how shall a man do otherwise and profess to trust his God?

Now, in about two hours the rear Truck of the Tender of the Locomotive jumped the track. And the Train was going fast, so that before it stopped it ran for more than its length, and the deep cuts of the Derailed Truck showed in the Ties behind the Train. And it was lucky that we were not Piled in an Heap.

And I walked forward to the Locomotive and stood beside the Conductor as he directed the Train Crew. And he gave them few orders, but when he spake they got busy and did as he said.

And I inquired of him, saying. Is thy Philosophy working well?

And he answered. Sure thing. We have everything to be thankful for. No one is hurt. The Truck is uninjured. The day is fine for outdoor work. And I have a Train Crew that can coax a recalcitrant Truck back on the track like Mary's Little Lamb.

And even as he spake, the Flanges returned to the Rails, and the Whistle blew for the Flagman, and the Conductor said. All Aboard.

Then did the Conductor come back and speak unto me, saying,

Thou art a Scholar. I am a Roughneck. But if I had thine Ability and thy Pulpit, then would I stand and speak unto men and women, saying.

Hearken unto me, and take good heed. Thine Imagination can depict no Heaven fairer than this Good Old World might be if ye would only take it at its best, and Trust God, and stop worrying. For which is worse, to be an Atheist and believe in no God, or to profess to believe in God and then distrust his care? Surely if there be any sin against the Holy Ghost is it not this, to profess to believe in the Guidance of God, and then to worry as if the Devil Owned the Planet and was keeping it for Home Consumption?

And I said unto him, Though thou call thyself a Roughneck, yet dost thou preach a Mighty Practical Gospel.

And he said. Yea, and I live it. Therefore have I on mine arm these many stripes, and in mine heart the song of youth and the joy of life. And it costeth very little, and the wealth of rubies is not to be compared unto it.

Now the Train had lost but Forty Minutes, which is not much more than it sometimes taketh to replace a Punctured Tire. But the Train sped on its way, and we pulled in On Time.

And I bowed before him as I left the Train, and shook his hand. And he said, A quiet mind tendeth to a level head. Therefore do we the more quickly get back upon the Rails, with good courage, and good steam pressure, and here we are.

And there we were, even as he said.

The Strawberry Sundae

I went unto the Shop where they sell Books; for I desired to buy a Book. And the daughter of the daughter of Keturah went with me. And we rode together on the Trolley Cars, and we had a good time.

And when we came to the place where they sell Books, then did I show her a Picture Book while I looked over the New Books. And I bought one or two.

And when we departed, she said unto me, Grandpa, wilt thou buy for me an Ice Cream Cone?

And I said, I will surely do so; and if thou shalt say. Please, then will I do even better.

And she said, Please.

And we came unto a place where they sell Sweets, and we went within.

And I said, Shall I buy for thee a Sundae?

And she said, I have never eaten a Sundae, but I should like it very much.

And I said. What flavor wilt thou have?

And she said, I desire Chocolate.

So I bought for her a Chocolate Sundae, but as for myself, I bought Strawberry. For I think the Strawberry is the next to the best Berry that the Lord ever made (the best being the Red Raspberry, which I like much).

So the little maiden ate her Chocolate Sundae, and liked it exceeding well. But she liked the Ripe, Rich, Red, Juicy Color of my Strawberry. So that she looked over now and then and almost wished that she had not ordered Chocolate. And when I saw that she was Interested, I ate slowly, so that when she had finished, I had only begun. And that was Rather Hard upon the little maiden.

Now, when she had finished, she clasped her little hands together, and she leaned her little round elbows on the table, and she rested her chin on her little clasped hands, and she looked over at my dish, and she said:

It looks so nice that I will not ask for any.

Now, when I heard that, I did smile. For I thought it the very prettiest way of asking for a thing I had ever heard.

And I thought of the people whose only way of asking God for things is to tease him, and say, Give me this, and be quick about it for Christ's sake.

For I wonder how any man doth dare to say for Christ's sake when he is asking something for his own sake, and whether it doth not sound unto the angels like swearing.

For of all the sins which good Christian men commit, it seemeth to me that among the gravest may be the undisguised selfishness of their prayers.

And I wondered how to teach Christian men and women to ask for things as prettily as the daughter of the daughter of Keturah asked for the Strawberry Sundae.

For I might just mention in closing that she got all the Strawberry Sundae she desired when she asked for it in that way.

The Traffic Cop and The Blind Man

I walked in the streets of a City, which was for greatness like unto Nineveh or Babylon. And I came unto a place where two ways met.

And the traffic was something fierce. And there stood in the middle of the street that ran north and south, and also in the middle of the street that ran east and west, a Guardian of the Public Welfare. And he was great of girth, and tall like Goliath of Gath. And he wore a Blue Coat with Brass Buttons. And on his hands were White Gloves, symbolic of the purity of the Municipal Government.

And he blew an Whistle one time. And all the east and west traffic stopped, and it piled up on both sides of the street as the Waters of the Red Sea rose up when Moses, the servant of God, stretched forth his hand upon them. But all the north and south traffic moved on.

Then did he blow his Whistle twice. And all the east and west traffic flowed through, while the north and south traffic stood in a heap like the waters of Jordan in the days of Joshua, the son of Nun. And the people who were going east and west went over dry-shod and in safety.

And presently all traffic stopped both ways, for the Whistle blew not, but the Traffic-Cop raised his right hand. And all the Teamsters and the Chauffeurs and the Mahouts and even some of the Women Shoppers stood and obeyed his Gesture.

And the Traffic-Cop left his place in the middle of the Intersection of the Two Streets, and walked across the Street unto the Curb. And I looked, and behold, a Blind Man. And he was standing upon the Curb, and he was Confused.

And the Policeman took him by the arm, and led him over. Neither did he say unto him. Step lively, please. But he led the Blind Man to the Opposite Curb, and made a way for him among the Women Shoppers, so that they stood back and let him through.

Then did the Traffic-Cop return unto his place, and blow his Whistle, and the tides of Commerce and of Humanity flowed on.

And there was not a Chauffeur who saw it who swore at the Cop, neither was there any who beheld it who reproved him. For they had been impatient of every other delay, but they willingly waited while he led a Blind Man to safety.

And I thought of the Immutable Decrees of God, and of the Laws whereby he doth govern the Universe, how they are as right as the One Whistle for the north and south traffic and the Two Whistles for the east and west traffic. But I had a suspicion, which in me is a mighty faith, that without violating any of his Immutable Laws, the Great God can somehow care for his own. Yea, I have lived long, and I have sometimes seen the evidence that God leadeth the blind by a way that he knoweth not, but in a right way, and a way that is better than he could choose for himself.

For the Apostle Paul hath said that the Policeman is a Minister of God, and I know not why one should not learn from him a sermon.

The Screens and the Shoes

In a certain Island in the Great Ocean, and if thou shalt inquire of me the name thereof I will not tell it unto thee; the inhabitants aforetime were Cannibals and Heathen. And there came a Missionary and taught them that they should worship the Living and True God, and they turned from their idols of wood and of stone. And afterward came a Merchantman; for wheresoever the Gospel doth go, there do men buy Spades and Spelling Books and Plows and Pianos and Pills. And he took his pay in Copra, and in the Oil of the Cocoanut and in Pearls.

And he found among the Natives a good market for nearly all of his stock save only for his Shoes. For the people of that Island had ever gone Barefoot, and they liked it not a Little Bit that they should be compelled to Cultivate Corns for which they had no need.

And they said, Behold, we were born barefoot, and so were our fathers.

But the Missionary builded a new House for the Worship of God, and it had a floor of Wood. And when he walked, then did his Shoes squeak. Likewise did the Shoes of the Missionary's Wife.

And the next day did the Chief of that Island and the Chief of his Wives come unto the Merchantman, and say, Sell unto us Shoes, and give us those that Squeak, and behold, here are Two Goodly Pearls.

And they picked out Shoes that squeaked much.

Then did that Merchant try on all his Shoes and readjust the Prices on the basis of Sound Business Psychology. For those Shoes that squeaked little did he mark up a little, but those that squeaked much, of those did he multiply the price.

Now the people wore Shoes only on the Sabbath, for the Shoes did not squeak in the Sand. Howbeit, in the Sanctuary, there did they squeak much, and Front Seats were at a Premium.

And the Merchantman sent a Letter by a Passing Steamer, and he ordered Many More Shoes.

But suddenly the Inhabitants ceased to buy Shoes. And the Merchantman knew not the reason. Therefore did he go to the Sanctuary upon the Sabbath. And he beheld how the people came with their Shoes under their arm, and put them on at the door of the Sanctuary, and wore them down the Aisle, and then removed them and passed them out of the Window for others to wear as they entered the House of God. For the Cooperative Idea had hit that Island, and it was nigh unto ruining business. For not only were there many Shoes on the way, but the Export Trade in Copra and Pearls and Cocoanut Oil did depend upon having something to sell that the people wanted.

So the merchantman considered. And shortly before the Ship was expected that was to bring his Shoes, he said unto the Missionary, Behold, the Windows of the House of God must be open to the winds, because the Climate is hot; but it is not seemly that they should admit Flies and Mosquitoes. Behold, I have long contemplated making a Gift to the Sanctuary; I will fit it out with Fly Screens.

And the Missionary was glad, and the Merchantman did even as he said, and he made the Wire Screens Very Tight, so that no Mosquito could get through, and how much less a Shoe.

Therefore did the Shoe Business revive on that Island, and it continueth good even unto this day.

This Parable might be used to teach that it doth ever reward a man to be generous toward the Sanctuary and to do those things that please the Preacher. But that is not the lesson, beloved.

Behold, the human mind is Queer, and men who seek the Truth, seek it for diverse reasons. There are those who desire Truth in the inward parts, and who buy the Truth for its own sake and sell it not. But others think they love the Truth who love the sound of Fine Phrases, and the use of words that feel good in the mouth. These are they that buy not the Shoe but the Squeak. And they are many. But be not thou like unto them; but rather let thy feet be shod with righteousness, and with the preparation of the Gospel of peace.

Things Not to Be Forgotten

I rode upon a Railway Train, Somewhere in Kansas, and the Train stopped Thirty Minutes for Lunch. And at one end of the Station was there a little Park, with two great Sun Dials, whereof one showed Central Time and the other showed Mountain Time. And the Park was attractive, and had Cost the Railway Some Coin, and the result was worth it.

Now there stood in the little Park, hard by the Train, a strong White Post, as it were two cubits in height. And there was framed in the top of the post an old-time Drawbar, with a Coupling-Pin and a Link. And upon the Post was painted in Black Letters this Superscription, Lest We Forget.

And I said unto myself. It may be that this is the town where the man lived who first invented the Safety Coupler.

And I entered the Station, and I inquired of the Young Man who was Clerk of the Station Hotel. And I asked of him, saying,

Wherefore is that Post with the old Drawbar erected in this Town rather than in another?

And he said. Where is it at? For I have never seen it.

And I inquired of another, and he said,

Thou mayest search me; for I have never noticed it.

And I inquired of the Station Agent, and he said,

I once knew, but, behold, I have forgotten.

Then did the Conductor say, All Aboard, and I got on board.

And I considered the days of my boyhood, when I played about the Cars, and I Knew Railway men; and many of them had lost fingers that were crushed in coupling cars; and many lost their hands, and others lost their lives.

And I said, Behold, there was a man who considered all these things, and sat up nights, and peradventure pawned his Shirt that he might invent a method of avoiding all this. And here is his memorial, marked, Lest We Forget; and some men pass it every day and never see it; and others once knew its meaning but they have forgotten.

And I looked out of the car window, and I beheld a Church, and upon the Church was a Spire, and upon the Spire was a Cross.

And I thought of the multitudes who continually pass it by, and I was grieved in mine heart; for I said. Among them are those who say, I have never seen it; and others say, I have seen it, but what it meaneth, behold, I know not. And others say, Behold, I once knew, but I have forgotten.

The Car Wheels

A certain man labored in the Division Terminal of a great Railway. And it was so that when a Train entered the Station, that there they changed Engines, and Train-crews. And certain men put Ice in the Coolers, and Water in the Tanks. And there were times when certain others swabbed the Windows so that they might be seen through; but this did not always occur. And the duty which was assigned unto this man was this, that he should begin at the head of the Train, and walk the length of it, and stoop down and strike every Car Wheel with a Hammer. And he did Precisely as he was told. For he walked the length of every train, and struck every wheel on the right side thereof, and then turned himself about and walked back upon the other side of the Train and the wheels upon that side did he strike in like manner. And this he did quickly, so that he had it done by the time other men had put Ice in the Coolers and Waste and Dope in the Boxes of the Axles, and the Engines had been changed. Now it came to pass that after many years the General Superintendent spake unto the President of the Road, and he said. Behold this man hath been on our Pay-roll for Five and Twenty years, and he hath never missed a day. Let us Celebrate, and Recognize his Faithfulness, and give him a Gold Watch, and a Pass for himself and his Wife unto California and back, and a little purse of Gold which he may blow in on a good time.

And they did even so.

And while the celebration was in progress some one asked of him, saying,

What is the reason why the wheels must be struck? And what is the occasion thereof?

And he said. Thou mayest search me. I know nothing save that I draw my pay for hitting the wheels, and I hit them every time and never miss a wheel.

But he had never listened to the ring of the hammer that he might hear whether the wheels were sound or cracked, neither had he known nor regarded. But he had done his job and drawn his pay for twenty-five years.

Now when I heard this tale, I said. That man is not so infrequent as some men might suppose. There are many who go through life in like manner. They do the day's job and draw their pay and never think what it all is for. Yea, there might even be such men in the pulpit, but may God forbid; and there are such in many another vocation.

And I prayed my God for all men, that they may labor, not only to strike the wheels but to listen for the ring.

For there are those who strike the wheels and go on, and if the Train run through, they say it is the result of Careful Supervision, and if the wheel crack, and the train land in the Ditch, they say it is a Mysterious Providence.

And there are such men, not a few, who obtain their living by labor no more intelligent than this, and some of them less continuous. And some of them travel on passes and receive the praise of men.

But God knoweth whether men listen for the ring, or whether they only hit the wheels.

Things Ancient and Modern

There came unto me a Lady who was an Enthusiast on Recent Things. And she spent her time in this, either to See or to Hear Some New Thing, even as did the women in Athens. And she inquired of me, saying,

Hast thou read the Modern Poetry? And dost thou not think that It is Just Too Lovely for Any Use?

And I said, I have read that which is called Modern Poetry. And some of it is Modern Poetry. And some of it is Modern but not Poetry; and some of it may be Poetry but it is not Modern; and some of it is neither Modern nor Poetry. As for its being Just too Lovely for Any Use, that is my opinion of the Major Part thereof; I have no Use for it.

And she inquired further, and said, Hast thou seen the Modern Dances?

And I answered and said, I have covered One Eye and Partly Closed the Other, and I have seen the Modern Dances.

And she said. Are they not Beautiful?

And I said, I can think of Several Adjectives which I would sooner apply to them.

And she said. Tastes Differ.

And I said, Tastes differ less than thou dost suppose. I went once unto the Circus of the renowned Phineas T. Barnum. And he had just imported a Cannibal Family from the Ends of the earth. And the man and the woman and the little boy lay upon a Platform, and were stolid and Homesick. Neither cared they whether people looked at them or not. But there came that way a little white boy with a small Red Balloon. And the little Cannibal boy leaped to his feet and ran to the edge of the Platform, and in heathenish Gibberish but with very Christian Tears he pleaded for it.

And I said. The tastes of that little Naked Heathen as to Red Balloons were Identical with those of the daughter of the daughter of Keturah, who hath been a Puritan for Ten Generations.

And I said. When Oscar Wilde was a popular fad, and every Dude wore a Sunflower in his Buttonhole, and the Civilized world attired itself in Pale Yellows and Discouraged Greens and Godforsaken Blues, we that were wise knew that it would not Last Very Long.

And she said, We were talking, I believe, of the Modern Dances.

And I said. There are three good things about the Modern Dances. The Position is so Objectionable, and the Dances are so Ungainly and the Musick is so Barbarous, that they will go where Oscar Wilde's color scheme hath gone.

And she said, Thou speakest not of their Morals, whereof I thought that thou wouldest speak.

And I said, I have been young, and I attribute not to young folk all the bad motives which rise in the mind of us Old Sinners. But the first of the Ten Commandments of Musick is, Thou shalt be Rythmickal; and the second is. Thou shalt be Melodious; and the third is. Thou shalt be Harmonious. Behold, there shall be a day when the Cowbells and the Clappers shall go to Grass, and the Fiddle shall play tunes as melodious as the good old Tunes of the Money Musk and Sugar in the Gourd.

And she said, But they will be Modern Tunes.

And I said. The Chinese do bury Eggs for an Hundred years and when they Exhume them, they count them the Freshest Things that ever Hens Laid. There are things that call themselves Modern which were Ancient when Lot's wife gave her coming-out party for her daughters. But the things that are Clean, and Wholesome and Lovely and of Good Report, these are the Ancient Things, and every generation will come to them at length as the things most Modern.

The Shoestrings

I went unto the shop of the man who selleth Shoes. And I said unto him. Sell unto me a pair of Good Shoestrings.

And he said, I will sell unto thee a pair of Shoestrings, but I will not promise to sell unto thee good ones. For the best of them are Mighty Poor these days, and most of them are Rotten.

And I said. These Flat ones with Metal tips I like not. Hast thou not some better ones?

And he said, I have some Round ones with Rubber tips, and they cost a Dime.

And I bought a pair.

Now of all the Shoestrings that ever were made, these were the Hardest and the most Slippery. And I tied them not once a day but it may have been Forty Times. And they slipped loose so that my feet slid to the front end of my shoes and grew Tender and Sore. And every morning I said, I will wear them this one day, and if they grow not better with the using, I will throw them away. But they grew no better. And I tried them another day. And I began to walk upon the side of my foot to ease it where it was sore. And in so doing, I caught my foot on a certain day as I crossed the street, and stumbled and was well-nigh run down by a swift chariot that had no regard for the Speed Limit.

And I went unto my home, and cast aside the round, hard strings, and I put in another pair that would stay tied. And I upbraided myself that I had endured for so long a time an evil that had as its only compensation of endurance the hope of getting value out of a pair of Shoestrings that cost a Dime.

Now it came to pass that I had occasion to use a Box. And I went unto the Attick and I found a Shoe Box, made of Pasteboard. And it was exactly what I wanted. And in it was Tissue Paper which had come wrapped about the Shoes. And I removed the paper, and behold, in the Box that I thought was empty, were two pairs of New Shoestrings, which I had bought with New Shoes in the good old days before the War, before Shoestrings were Rotten. And I rejoiced as one who findeth Coin.

Now I considered these things, and I said within myself, Even so do men endure Petty Abuses and Small Annoyances and even Greater Wrongs, whose aggregate of Discomfort is Great, and whose liability of Danger is not Inconsiderable, and whose hope of amendment is Small and whose Value is Negligible. And they submit to them when they ought to face them and remedy them. Yea, and thus do men continue with Faults of their own, which seem small, but which Irritate and do Harm out of proportion to all the effort that would be necessary to their amendment. Yea, and when they know not wherewith to amend these evils, behold the remedy lieth under their own roof, and is already bought and paid for and ready to their hand.

Wherefore, search thine Attick, and bring forth out of it all the unused resources that may minister to life, and use them. For of what use is it that thou walk with Sore Feet when there is a good new pair of Pre-war Shoestrings in the Empty Shoe Box in thine Attick?

And now if thou shalt behold me walking down the Highway, with a quick step and a smiling countenance, know ye that the reason is that my feet are shod with the Preparation of the Gospel of Peace, and that I wear Shoestrings that do not slip. For the Lord maketh the feet of the righteous like unto Hinds' Feet; but of the sinner and the ungodly is it said, Their feet shall slide in due time.

The Lost Tooth

The daughter of the daughter of Keturah came unto our habitation, and she sought the Cookie Box of Keturah. And thus did Keturah's own children in their day. And thus have I done often. Save that I never eat one Cookie. I can eat none and I can eat four or five, but I cannot eat one of the Cookies of Keturah and stop. And the little maiden ate of the Cookies of Keturah. And I think that there will always be Cookies in her Cookie Box.

Now as the damsel ate, she cried out in terror.

And I wondered what had happened unto her, for that is not the way the Cookies of Keturah affect people.

And she cried not in pain, but in terror. And she said, Oh, Grandpa, my tooth has come out!

And she held up a tiny front tooth in her little hand.

Now the loss of a Tooth is a matter of some importance to me; for I fear lest the time come when the grinders cease because they are few. But I knew that for her it was not a serious matter.

And I comforted her, and I said, Fear not. It is of no consequence.

And she said, Oh, Grandpa, canst thou put it back?

And I told her that I could not, and that I would not if I could.

And she understood it not, but she was comforted when she saw that I did not share her fear.

And I said. Have no fear, my little girl. The teeth that God gave thee when teeth first came unto thee, were baby teeth, and they will leave thee one by one, and fall out. Trouble not thyself, for there shall grow others in their place that will be stronger and better and last longer.

And she was comforted.

Then I considered the losses of life, and the pain and the fear of them, and how they are even as the fear that was in the heart of the little maiden when she lost the Tooth. Yea, I went where people suffered by reason of losses which I could not explain so easily, and my words of comfort had behind them no knowledge of what blessing God should provide instead of the thing that had been taken away.

But I remembered that it is written in the Word of God how God hath provided Some Better Thing.

And I took the little pearly tooth from the hand of the little maiden, and she sat upon my knee and ate the residue of her Cookie, and I stroked her Golden Hair, and I prayed unto God for all those who have losses in life and who know not how God shall provide any better thing in place of them.

For their sorrow is like unto the sorrow of the daughter of the daughter of Keturah, and there are times when my wisdom stoppeth short of their need.

The Transformed Tooth

The daughter of the daughter of Keturah lost a Tooth. And she carried it about in her hand, and she showed it with great Pride. And she said. Behold the Tooth which I had, and which came out this morning. And behold, here is the place where it grew, and another shall grow in its place; for thus hath my Grandpa told me.

Now she showed it unto one who said unto her,

Wrap thou the Tooth in Paper, and put it under thy Pillow tonight, and it will turn into a Dollar.

And she came home and told her mother. And she said. Here is a piece of Paper, and I will wrap my Tooth in it; and in the morning the Tooth will be gone, and in its place will there be a Dollar.

And her mother could not permit that the little maiden should break her heart or suffer disappointment; therefore did she not forbid it.

And after the little maiden was asleep, then her mother considered what was best to be done.

And in the morning the little damsel awoke, and she felt under her Pillow, and behold, there was no tooth there, but a Dollar.

And she ran down the stairs, and she cried with a loud voice, saying. Behold, mother, what hath happened; for my Tooth hath turned into a Dollar.

And she took the money to the Bank and added to her Savings Account.

And the little damsel considered, and she asked of her mother and inquired, saying, How many teeth have I?

And her mother said. Thou hast Twenty and Four.

And she asked, Will they all come out?

And her mother answered, Yea, and more will grow in their place.

Then began the little maiden to consider how that she could Support the Family with the Unearned Increment from her Teeth. For she said. Mother, I have twenty and four teeth, and every one of them shall turn into a Dollar. Consider how Rich we shall be.

And her mother told it unto me.

And she asked, Ought I to have told her that the Tooth turneth not into a Dollar, and that her friend lied unto her? For behold, these are the days of the High Cost of Living; and if I am in for twenty and four dollars to provide the means for this transformation, that is a little more money than I contemplated.

And I said. Trouble not thyself. The little maiden will face quite soon enough the stern, hard facts of life. Deprive her not of her little happy illusions, nor seek to fetter too soon with the shackles of Grim Reality the precious gift of the Imagination. For this is the gift of God, and we of this age do too much clip its wings. Behold, here is a Dollar into which the next Tooth may be transformed, and when thou seest another Tooth working loose, come again to thy father.

For the little maiden hath learned a very precious thing, which is to make an asset of one's losses, and to transform the vacant interstices of life into opportunities of larger promise. I would she could teach unto all humanity that if it will lay its losses under its pillow, and go to sleep with faith in God, the night worketh a wonderful transformation, and joy Cometh in the morning. For this is my hope, even when I lay away not a Tooth only but the body of which the Tooth is a part, that the day shall dawn and the shadows flee away. For His is the image and superscription upon the coinage of that into which life's losses are convertible in the morning of the new day.

And I shall be satisfied when I awake with His likeness.

The Minister and the Saw

Now there came to me one of the sons of the Prophets, even a young minister, and he said, My church treateth me harshly.

And I said. What hast thou done to thy Church?

And he said, I upbraided them, and I told them they were Miserable Sinners.

And I answered, Thou didst speak truthfully and unwisely.

And he said, Is it not wise to speak the truth?

And I said, It is not wise to speak anything else; but Truth is precious, and should be used with Economy.

And he said, There were Great Reforms that needed to be wrought in that Town, and a Great Work to be done, and I had hoped to Inspire the Church to Do Those Things. But they are Stiff-necked, and they seek to Fire me.

And I said to him. Come with me into my Garden.

And we went out into the Garden, and I took with me a Saw.

And I said. Climb thou this tree, for thou art younger than I.

And he climbed the Tree, and sat upon a Limb thereof as I showed him.

And I said. That limb needeth to be Cut Off. Take thou the saw and Cut it Off.

And he began to saw beyond him.

And I said, Saw on the other side.

And he began to saw, but he stopped, and he said, If I saw the limb between myself and the Tree, I shall surely fall.

And I said unto him. The minister who pusheth a Reform faster than his Church will follow him, and findeth himself Fired, is like unto the man who Ascendeth a Tree, and Saweth off a Limb between himself and the Tree.

And I left him there, and I went into mine House. And he sat there Some Little Time in Deep Meditation.

And he Climbed Down, and returned to his own Church. And he called the elders thereof together, and he said, I have been foolish, and have sought to Bring in the Millennium Before Sundown. Be patient with me, and I will strive to be more patient with the Church.

And they answered and said, Now thou art Talking like a man of Sense. Continue thou to chasten us for our sins, and show us how to be better, but expect not the Impossible, and lo, we will stand by thee till the Cows Come Home.

And the minister whom the Church was about to Fire took thought, and added a Cubit to his Stature; and his Church Rallied about him, and the last I heard some of the things he wanted to Get Done were being done.

And he wrote me a letter, saying,

O Safed, thou didst have me Up a Tree, but behold I am down and on the Job, and if thou wouldst see a happy and united and hustling Church, where the people love their minister, and the minister loveth his people, and where everything is up and moving, and good is being done, come over and see us.

And I read the letter and rejoiced. For there are Ministers who have learned How to Saw, but neither When nor Where. And if they will Climb my Apple Tree I will teach them wisdom.

The Transplanted Pine

Where I go in Summer, there grow trees, and there is an hill where men dig out Gravel. And there was a Young Pine Tree that grew upon the top of the Gravel Hill, above the Pit. And the earth had fallen away from beneath it, so that it fell down into the Pit, and it clung to the earth above by a Single Root. And thus had it hung for many weeks.

Now my sons came home, and we rejoiced to see them, and they sojourned with me and Keturah for a few days. And one of them came from the Army and another came from the Navy, and another came from the Balloons that fly above the ships, for it was a time of war.

And my four sons put on Old Clothes, and they inquired of me, saying. What shall we do that is too hard for thee? For thus do my sons speak unto me.

And I said, Bring out the Wheelbarrow, and the Spade and the Mattock, and come with me.

And when they saw the Tree, they said. Shall we transplant it? But surely it will not live?

But they said, Let us give unto the Boss no Back-talk. If our father desireth any old thing, that will we do.

And I said. Boys, I think that we may waste our labor; nevertheless, I desire to give unto the tree a chance for its life.

So we found a place for it, and we digged an hole, and we digged out the one root that held the tree. And we placed the root thereof on the Wheelbarrow, and we planted it.

And it was in August. And certain of the neighbors said. Hast thou not Pine Trees enough? Behold, thy woods are full of them. And this one will surely die.

Now we went away, and in a year we came again. For the war ended, and my sons returned, for which I thank my God daily.

And behold, the Pine Tree died not, but grew. And though it had but one root in the ground when we took it up, and the time was Summer, yet did it live; yea, and it still liveth. And its height is twelve cubits, and its thickness is the thickness of the arm of a man.

And I stood beside the Pine, and I spake unto it, saying, Thou mayest well thank me and thy Lucky Stars, and my Four Sons that thou didst not perish in the Horrible Pit and the Sliding Gravel.

And the Pine Tree said unto me, I owe unto thee my life, but I did not ask thee for it, and I know not yet whether I shall thank thee. But if thou desirest me to grow, then do thou make it possible for me to grow. Let not my root be smothered with growing Brush, nor permit the Scrub Oak to shut me out from the Blue Sky and the Blessed Sun.

And I considered that Life is not enough; for there should be also something that shall make Life worth living and Growth and Joy possible.

And I prayed unto my God on behalf of all men whose lives are shut in so that they have little place for their root nor much opportunity of seeing the blessed Sun. For what the Pine needeth do they need.

The Value of Things Despised

Now There is an Handmaiden of the Lord whom I know and Honor, and she had an Accident, so that her Arm was Bound Up in a Sling. And I went to see her that I might Comfort her in her Affliction.

And I found her very Cheerful, for such is her Wont.

And I asked her what ailed her Arm, and she answered that she thought it was a Sprain, but that the Physician had given it a name such as Physicians give unto the ills of people who can afford it. And he told her that it would be well in a Fortnight or Thereabout, but meantime to be Careful, and look well to her Diet, and have a Specialist examine her Tonsils, and have an X-Ray made of her Teeth. For such is the habit of Physicians.

And I said, I am glad that it will soon be well. Meantime, be thou thankful that it is thy Left Hand.

And she answered and said, O Safed, art thou a Wise man, and hast thou nothing better to say to me? Behold, I have learned a better lesson than that.

And I asked her, What is the Lesson?

And she said, I am finding every blessed minute of the day how few things I can do with my Right hand alone. Wherefore, I am thanking God that all these years I have had a good Left hand, as well as a Right.

And I meditated, and I said. Thou hast well said. Well would it be for us all if we could learn thus the value of the things we despise.

For the Right Hand is from God, and so also is the Left; and he who loveth his Right Hand should not forget to thank God that He hath given him the Left Hand also.

The Flesh and the Spirit

There came unto me one of the Sons of the Prophets; and he was a goodly young man. His Brow was High and Pale, and so was the rest of him. And he took himself Seriously, which is not a Bad Thing to do if one work not over-time on the job.

And forasmuch as Keturah had other fish to fry on that day, I took him to Luncheon at a Restaurant.

And he looked upon the bill of fare and heaved a sigh. And he said, I have to be Very Careful of my Eating.

And he spake unto the Waitress, and he said, Give me a Very Thin Slice of Toast, and a Very Soft Boiled Egg, and a Cup of Hot Water.

Now I thought that it would do him good to receive a Little Jolt.

And I spake unto the Waitress, and I said, Bring unto me a Thick, Juicy Beefsteak, and a Baked Potato with a Trap Door in the Top, and a Chunk of Butter in the Trap Door, and some Paprika sprinkled round about the Butter; and bring unto me also a Cup of Coffee, and a Quarter Section of Hot Mince Pie with the Bark On, and a Slice of Cheese with the Pie.

And the Waitress smiled a Little Subjective Smile, for she knew that I did not always go in quite so Heavy, and she surmised that it was an Object Lesson. But she spake nothing, save that she said, Yessir. And she departed.

And the young man was Astonished.

And he said, Thou art a man with Gray Hair, yet dost thou give thought to what thou shalt eat and drink.

And I said. That is just where thou dost fool thyself. It is thou who givest thought to it. For thou dost ever consider what thou shalt eat and what thou must not eat; whereas I think not of it at all; but when I come to the Table, then do I eat, and give God thanks that I have food and good digestion.

And he said. With such an Appetite, I wonder thou art not dead long since.

And I said. Thou wilt be dead before thou art half my age if thou forget not to think about thy Digestion.

And I said unto him. My son, hearken unto me, and learn wisdom. It is not for nothing that the Good God hath put our Stomach and all the Organs thereunto appertaining out of our sight. It is not the overloading of the stomach that killeth men so much as the overloading of the mind. I am this day eating more than is my wont; but I shall get away with it, and thou wilt have Nervous Indigestion over thy Nursing Bottle Stuff.

And I said unto him, Rise early in the morning. Get a little exercise before Breakfast. Eat lightly but sufficiently, and get in a good morning's work. Get out in the afternoon, and make thy Parish Calls on foot, and make about five times as many of them as thou art now making. Then shalt thou come to the table with such appetite that thou couldst eat an Horse with the Harness on. Eat heartily, yet not as a Glutton. Leave the table while thou art still Capable but not Desirous. As for the kind of food which thou devourest, eat what is set before thee and ask no questions, save it be for a second helping. It is not that which goeth into a man which causeth indigestion, but the evil thoughts of whether it is safe for me to eat this or that or so much. The man who preacheth hath need of a good flow of Red Blood. For him a Beefsteak is a means of Grace. And when thou hast eaten and art full, give thanks to God; and as for thy Digestion, Forget It.

Now in after days he came again to me, and he said, To see a man of thine age consume a Beefsteak and a Hot Mince Pie was to me of more worth than half that I learned in the School of the Prophets.

And I beheld that he was no longer Pale, but a sure enough Man.

The Hornets' Nest

When Summer cometh, I and Keturah we leave the City behind us, and we go Far From the Madding Crowd to a place where there are Trees and a Little Lake. And the trees of the Lord are full of sap, and also full of Birds and Squirrels and such like things. And we suffer no man to harm them; yea, our children spent their summers there, and played among them and made friends of them and harmed them not.

Now when we arrived at the beginning of this summer, behold, there was a great Nest of Hornets in one of the trees hard by the house. And it was certain days before we saw it.

Then came to us certain who said, Destroy it, for it will make thee trouble.

And they said, Know ye that these are no Nice Little Yellow Jackets with a Gentle Sting; for these be the Regular Old Fashioned Big Black Fellows, with a sting about an Inch Long; and the way they sting is Something Fierce; and when one of them cometh after a fellow, then do they all come, and settle upon him so that he is Black with them, and sting him mightily.

And I said. Those hornets saw us several days before we saw them, and they troubled us not. So long as they behave like Gentlemen or Ladies or whichever they ought to be, I will harm them not.

So we let them alone.

And I and Keturah we watched them as they went in and out of the many holes of their Nest. For the Nest was larger than the head of a man. And they worked so that compared to them the Little Busy Bee is a Sluggard. And they paid no manner of attention to us. Yea, we came near and beheld, and they went on about their business.

And I considered how foolish it had been to try to destroy the Nest; for then had they stung us; yea and those that escaped had remained and come at us daily until either we or they were driven out.

But the good God hath given unto them some measure of the joy of life, and they menace us not save as we trouble them.

Wherefore did we mind our own business, and the hornets did the same. Neither did we in all the summer get one sting, or have one hornet fly at us.

And I considered how many men there are who continually Hunt Trouble. For whenever they see any sort of thing that doth irritate them, then do they throw a club at it and get stung good and plenty. And then do they come with a pole and a rag soaked in coal oil and get stung some more. And so it goeth with them all through life. Whereas there is a More Excellent Way.

For both I and the Hornets we minded our own business. And the Hornets are still there. And no man molesteth them or maketh them afraid.

This parable teacheth that it is well for a man that he mind his own business.

Heroes and Heroines

There came to me a man and a woman, even a Husband and his Wedded Wife, and they said, We are weary one of the other.

And I said. Why is it thus?

And they said, We have grown commonplace to each other. Once we were to each other a Hero and an Heroine, but now we are Neither.

And I said, Napoleon did not look heroic to Josephine after she had seen him with his Suspenders hanging down his back; neither did Joan of Arc look heroic when she held her Front Hair in her mouth while she did up her back hair.

And they said. But he was an Hero and she was an Heroine.

And I said. Heroes and Heroines cannot appear heroic all the time. Caesar did not look heroic when he had pushed his slippers too far back under the bed, and he had to get down and fish them out with an umbrella; but that be a necessary thing, even to Heroes and Heroines.

And I said to the woman, When the Baby was sick, eight years ago, did not this thine Husband watch with thee day and night?

And she said. He did.

And I said unto the man, When thou hadst lost half thy money in a Fool Speculation, did she not stick by thee like a Little Burr, and cheer thee up, and never say, I told thee so?

And he said. It is even so.

And I said, Go down on your knees.

And they knelt.

And I said, Join hands.

And they did so.

And I prayed to God on their behalf, till there came to their eyes tears of Memory and Love.

And I Smote them lightly on the back, and I said, I dub thee an Hero; I dub thee an Heroine.

And I sent them forth.

And they lived happily ever afterward.

Good Health and Veracity

I met a man, and I saluted him and said. Good Morning.

And he answered me with a Grunt.

And I said unto him, It is a Fine Day.

And he said, It may be, but I feel Sick.

And I said. According as thou feelest, so art thou.

And he said, A fellow cannot help feeling bad when he doth feel bad.

And I said, Thou art most surely wrong.

And I said. Where dost thou feel ill?

And he said, I was out late last night at a Party, and I went to bed Two Whole Hours later than usual, and I slept but a Half Hour later than I commonly do, and I rushed for my train. Therefore doth my Head Ache and I feel ill.

And I said unto him, How many arms hast thou, and do they ache?

And he said, They are all right and their number is Two.

And I said, How many fingers hast thou on each hand, that would pain thee if any one of them were cut or broken?

And he said, I have ten fingers, but I see not what that has to do with it.

I said unto him. Take heed to what I say and learn wisdom. The two hours of sleep that thou didst lose are something, but not much. It is thine extra half hour in bed that aileth thee. Thou shouldest have risen a little earlier than usual and burned a little more Oxygen. If thine head felt Rocky, thou shouldest have said, I have two good legs, which are all right, and I will stretch them with a little walk. I have two good Arms, and I will swing them. I have two good Eyes and I will fill them with the Beauty of the Morning. I have two good Lungs, and they pain me not; I will cram them with Fresh Air. I have two good Ears, and never an Earache; I will listen to the Birds as I walk.

And I said unto him, I am accustomed to going to bed two hours later than usual. It is not the loss of sleep that hurteth a man if he lose a little more in getting fresh air.

And he said, Thou speakest words of folly. If a man lose sleep, he must make it up; and if he feeleth ill, there is no reason why he should lie about it.

And I said. According as a man thinketh in his heart so is he well or ill. The good God who made this world hath put into it that wherewith we may be strong, and he who riseth in the morning with a heavy feeling in his head ought to have more sense than to lie later than usual and gorge his breakfast and run for the train, and then blaspheme his God by telling the world that he feeleth ill.

And he said, It is just possible that thou speakest a little bit of good sense, and I have not considered it before.

And I said unto him, Consider it now, and it shall be worth more than an whole Apothecary Shop to thee.

Failure and Success

Keturah made a Cake. And the manner of making it was this. She baked it in Three Sections, and when they came from the Oven, she laid them one upon another so that the Cake was Three Stories in Height. And between the layers she placed Frosting, yea, and more Frosting upon the top thereof. And into the Frosting did she put handfuls of meat out of the Cocoanut. For there be many kinds of cake that I like, even every kind that Keturah doth make, but the best of all is the kind that is made with Cocoanut.

And when she served the Cake, she said, Alas, my lord, it is a Failure.

And I said, Wherefore should it be a Failure?

And she answered. The Telephone did ring just when the Frosting should have been attended to, and it hath not sufficiently hardened. Yea, it is Sticky, and a Failure.

And when I beheld it, lo, very much of the Frosting had run down the sides of the Cake. Nevertheless, there was much of it still upon the top, and between the layers, and the Cocoanut was all to the Good.

And I said. Since it is a Failure, it were well to eat more of it, and put the Poor Thing out of Sight.

And Keturah said. Thou hast well said. Eat thou another slice, and yet another.

And I did as I was bidden. And albeit the Cake was a trifle Sticky, there was nothing else that was not one hundred per cent, to the good.

Therefore, when she maketh something that is Unusually Good, I say unto her, Is not this a Failure? For I desire another piece.

And I would that we might somehow readjust life that all life's Failures might somehow make for success. Yea, I remember that my God hath promised that in some way that I know not the wrath of man shall praise him.

For if this world, which is a cake not turned, can scrape some of the char from its overdone side, and bake the side that is dough so that it can be eaten, then shall I rejoice. For I would believe that this world is a success, and by faith I so accept it.

The Bed and the Mattress

I journeyed unto a distant City. And I made a Speech. And I tarried there until the next day.

And one of the principal citizens invited me unto his home. And I went with him, and he entreated me well.

Now when he had shown me unto my Room, I beheld that all the Furniture was of Solid Mahogany. And the Bedstead was a Work of Art. But when I laid my Weary Form upon the Bed, I sought to sleep, and I could not. For the Mattress also was of Solid Mahogany, or something quite as Uncomfortable, and with Knots in the Mahogany. And the Spring sagged, so that it deposited me in an Heap in the middle of the Bed, and I required a Derrick wherewith to get out of it.

Now the good God, who made the Trees, made them of many kinds, and the Wood of those trees hath each of them its own variety of Beauty. And I love the color of Mahogany, even when I suspect that it is Birch with a Stain upon it. But when I go unto my Bed, I soon forget the color of the wood, and I desire a Good Mattress and a Comfortable Spring.

And I considered concerning mine Hospitable Hosts that they had had about Fifty Dollars wherewith to buy a Bedstead and Spring and Bed for their Guest Room, and they had spent Forty of it for the Bedstead, and divided the Ten which they had left between a Sagging Spring and a Solid Mahogany Mattress with Lumps in It.

Now I considered that there are other people who do likewise. For I went unto the House of God, and there rose a Preacher, and he Preached. But he had put Forty Dollars of his Preparation into the Framework of his Sermon, and had only Ten Dollars and Five Minutes left wherein to Preach the Gospel.

And I called upon a man who was not a preacher, and I found that he was putting Forty Dollars of his Energy into Getting a Living, and less than ten dollars into the actual business of Living.

And I thought about the Solid Mahogany Bed and Mattress, and I said. The people who read these Parables are High Brow, and they want no Parables made out of such Homely and Commonplace Things. But I opened the book of the Prophet Isaiah, and I found there the words that he said,

The bed is shorter than that a man can stretch himself upon it, and the covering narrower than that he can wrap himself in it.

And I knew that Isaiah was a tall man, even as I, and that when the bedclothes pulled out at the foot, he could make a Parable out of it for the Highbrow people of Jerusalem. And I thought I would take a chance at it.

For there are many people in life who put too much into the Mahogany Bedstead and not enough into the Mattress and the Spring.

Proteids and Calories

We went, I and Keturah, unto a Feast. And the Feed was good, but the talk about it was Indecent. For the women talked of how to prepare a meal that had in it a requisite number of Calories and Carbohydrates and other suchlike Immodest things, and the men talked about how Gladstone gave unto each bite of Steak Thirty and Two Chews and how Horace Fletcher chewed Seventy-three times upon One Bean.

And after they had talked this subject out, and then some, one of them said. Why is Safed silent? For we have not often known it thus.

And I answered them not.

And they pressed me, and asked me if I felt not well.

And I said. There be three things which I like not; yea, four do I abominate. The first is Scandals. And the next is Anything which giveth unto one man a chance to Monopolize the Conversation, particularly if he be another than myself. And the third is stories of ocean travel which some fool doth always bring around to a story about Seasickness. And the last and most Indecent is talk about Digestion and Calories and other Infamies.

And they said, But surely it is meet that a man should know what goeth into his food, and whether it be wholesome?

And I said, It is better for him to marry a woman like Keturah, and trust her, and to keep himself ignorant about everything save that it tasteth mighty good and doth not cost more than his income.

And one of the women said. We are all studying about Foods and Balanced Rations, and it is natural that we speak of it when food is being eaten.

And I said, I would not have you ignorant of Calories, nor would I have a Physician ignorant of Gizzards and Spleens, but I would forget them at the Table.

Now by this time the Conversation had gotten to where I might monopolize it, and I said,

Eating is not a Pretty Exercise. Dogs do carry away the bone, and gnaw it aloud and growl. But man hath learned to sit down at the table opposite to another man and not be disgusted at the sight. Yea, and I count it a high reach of Civilization when we can eat decently together. But as for talking of the Constituent Parts of Food, I abhor it. I eat Food, not Calories; good, well-cooked, well-served, appetizing Eats, not Carbohydrates.

And I said, The dear Lord Christ rejoiced that men at Table could talk of things other than food. And he took Bread and Drink and said, This do, in remembrance of me.

And they said, Wouldest thou then that we talk only of Religion at the Table?

And I said, Religion for me is the whole of Normal Life, and I would talk of all things Fine and High and Friendly and Mirthsome, for so the good Lord would have us do. But I would eat and give God thanks and forget about Calories and Digestion.

And one of the men swore a Great Oath, and he said. By Heck, thou art right. I am Fed Up on this Calory Stuff. Let us cut it out.

And they all said, From this time forth all talk of Scandal, or Seasickness or of things relating to Food and its Digestion is Taboo.

And one of them said, Was there not a fourth?

And the hostess replied, There was, but that would be hard on Safed. Therefore will we not include it.

The Doughboy and the Kitten

I have witnessed no exhibition of Ardor chastened with Prudence more evident than is evinced by a Discharged Doughboy at a Special Sale of Shirts, having Sixty Dollars in his pocket, and remembering that besides the Shirts he must have a Suit.

And I beheld such an one on his way to procure his Citizens' Clothes, and he walked with a brisk step, with a stride such as he learned in the Fields of Flanders.

Now the street through which he passed had houses that were built solidly the one against the other, but each had a Small Dooryard in the front of it, with a Gate and a Brick Walk that led from the Door down to the Street.

And there stood at the Door of one of the houses a Small Kitten. And it pleaded piteously that it might enter. But there was none that regarded, neither any that opened the Door.

And the Doughboy turned upon his Heel as he had been the Pivot Man in a Left Wheel, and he turned to the Left, and he opened the Gate, and he walked down the Brick Walk, and rang the Bell. And when the Door was opened, then did he hand in the Kitten, and Salute, and walk away.

And I know not whether the Lady of the House liked it or not but she received the Kitten into the House, and did not shut it out.

And the Doughboy went on his way unto the Shirt Sale.

And when I saw him do that, I wished for him that he had money enough left over to buy him an Extra Good Striped Silk Shirt and a Four Dollar Necktie, besides those that he had money to buy. For I like that kind of a Doughboy.

Now I thought of the habits of men, and how many there be who are so engrossed with their own Troubles, and so cumbered with the cares of life, that they never have time to see any kittens at other people's doors, and see them at their own only that they may drive them away, and who look with little concern upon the sorrows of their fellow men as they pass on their way to Mill or to Market.

And I said, It would do a great many men an Whole Lot of Good as they march straight down the walk of Life, if they would look now and then to the right or the left, and behold the needs of other living creatures, and do for them the little deeds that cost but little and brighten the day.

For there are other creatures besides kittens that wail at unopened doors; and some of us could open some of them, and still get to the Shirt Sale in time to spend all the money that we have. But the day would be brighter for some one, and no darker for ourselves.

And a little later I passed the place where they sold Shirts, and the Doughboy was coming out, with a Good Big Package under his arm. And I blessed him in mine heart.

The Pianola

Of stupidity in men full grown have I seen not a little, and for some of it have the owners deserved great credit; for only by profound study of the business of being stupid could they have become as stupid as they are. But it goeth to mine heart to see in little children any manner of infirmity. Therefore am I saddened when I go to Public Institutions for Children, yet glad that such things be for the children who have need of them. And one such institution there is for children that are Feeble Minded. And I saw therein what they endeavor to do for children in whom the good God appeareth to have forgotten to make minds.

And among the rest was one who could play upon a Pianola.

And he did take rolls of Paper with Holes punched through, and tread with his feet, and the thing made musick.

And it was good musick, because the Rolls were good. But he knew not the Unfinished Symphony of Schubert from There'll be an Hot Time in the Old Town Tonight. But whatsoever was on the Roll, he played it. And to his feet it was good exercise, and to his mind it was a Pleasant Noise.

And I spake to the Superintendent and I said, Behold, I have enjoyed the musick, albeit the child that made the musick knew not that it was musick.

And I thought much. And I remembered men who make noises with their mouths which to them are Great Wisdom, and to the rest of us but Noise, and how with them the effect is the reverse of what doth happen when a Simple Child doth tread out with his feet musick which he knoweth not as such.

And I said to the Superintendent, It were well if thou didst have here certain men who are wise in their own eyes, and whose words are empty of wisdom. Then mightest thou treat them with the system. And if peradventure thou couldst work that system backward for their benefit, then might they hear how foolish are their own words. And it might be in time that they could make their heads as effective as the feet of a foolish boy.

But the Superintendent was not sure that his System could be worked backward.

The Unidentified Taste

I was once a Lad, and I loved Candy. And the Candy of that day came not in Boxes at a Dollar and the Half of a Dollar for a Pound, else had I never seen any of it with a Telescope. But it came in Sticks. And the price of a Stick of Candy was a Cent. And if one had great wealth, then might he obtain six sticks for Five Cents. But I seldom had Six Sticks.

Now there came unto our house a Visitor who brought unto us a small Paper Bag of Candy of another Sort. And it was of many sorts. And I ate one of the lumps, and it was more delicious than anything that I had ever eaten, or have eaten since.

It was not hard, but was more nearly soft; yet it was not utterly soft and squashy; but it had in it shreds of a substance with a flavor of its own, and it grated upon the teeth with a most celestial sensation. It gave unto the sense of taste a New Experience as of something that might have been contained in a Story Book, but never known in Real Life. It left in my mouth a Reminiscent Longing, mingled with a Happy Consciousness that I had experienced something finer of its kind than ever before had occurred to me.

Now as the years went by, and as I ca.me to know more about the various Kinds of Candy, I bought many kinds. For I love Chocolate Creams, and Cream Patties, and Divinity Fudge and divers other kinds, and I think that I shall always care for it. And I sought for many years for a kind of Candy that should taste as did that piece which I ate in my boyhood, but I found it not.

And it hath sometimes occurred to me that it may have been Cocoanut Bar that I ate, and knew not the name of it. But I have eaten much Cocoanut Bar and it is good, but it tasted not as that tasted.

So it seemeth that I shall go through life desiring that I may once again taste something as good as that which I once tasted, and that I shall not taste it again.

For, if it be so that what I ate was Cocoanut Bar, and I have eaten other since as good, then do I surely know that it was something in me that hath been lost, and not anything in the Candy. For I can never bring to it the appetite of a Boy, though mine is a Close Approach unto it.

And I considered the men who scold their wives because they cannot cook as those men's mothers did. And I consider that their wives are better cooks than their mothers, but that the men of jaded appetites bring no longer to the table the hunger of a boy, that is able to transform very ordinary cooking into something marvelously good. And I advise those men not to demand of their wives such cooking as mother produced until they saw wood long enough to get an appetite such as mother's darling little boy was used to possess.

But if there be any good woman who maketh Home Made Candy, and who can make me some that shall taste like that which I ate in that day when I was a boy, I would saw wood for some time for the joy of having that taste again in my mouth.

But if I never have it again, then shall no man take away from me that, or any joy that I once have had. For those joys are mine own forever.

The Keeper of The Inn

I lighted upon a certain place, and lodged there, I and Keturah. For there was an Inn in that place that was famous, and the master of the Inn had written unto me, saying. Come thou and bring Keturah, and lodge in mine Inn, and it shall not cost thee a Cent.

And when I arrived, behold there were people before the desk who were standing in line, and the Clerk was saying. We have no room, but are full to the Roof. And they were offering Big Money for any old place to sleep in this Inn. But unto me and Keturah did he give a Swell Room and Bath. And he said. Fret not thyself on account of the demand for Rooms, but stay as long as thou canst.

Now I talked with the master of the Inn, and I said, There be men who say of thee that thou art Visionary, and a Dreamer of Dreams; while others say that thou art a Cold Calculator, and that thou chargest to Advertising thine Art Gallery and thy Musick Hall and all the rest wherewith thine Inn is adorned. Tell me, I pray thee, on the level, how much of this is Idealism, and how much is straight Business?

Then he answered me and said. Forty and four years ago did my mother open an Hotel on this lot, and I was a lad who Peeled Potatoes, and Hustled Baggage and Ran Errands, and I grew up to the Business. And I have always been in Debt up to my Neck, and have always lacked Fifteen Cents of having enough money to do anything that I wanted to do. And I never dared to dream any Dreams that would not be accepted as Collateral at the Bank, or yield a net revenue of less than Six Per Cent. Fool not thyself with any notion that I am in this Business for my Health. My best advertisement is not mine Art Gallery but my Kitchen, which is open to all comers and where all may see just what goeth into the Soup Kettle. And my next-best advertisement is not my Musick Room but my Dining Room, with no spots on the Table Linen, and no dead flies in the food.

But if I can manage the Boarding-House Business so that there is in it a touch of Romance, and a Pleasing Suggestion of Musick and Art, what doth it matter whether I be a Dreamer or a Mercenary Scoundrel, so long as the Bank is getting its Interest, and Guests plead for rooms in mine Inn?

And I said. At least it mattereth to thine own heart.

And he said, A man who is in Business must be honest, or move frequently; and in my Business, removal is inexpedient. It is cheaper to be honest than to move. And it may be cheaper to maintain a Court of the Birds and an Art Gallery than to have Vacant Rooms, or to spend much money for Advertising.

And he said, I like Musick, and so doth my wife; and Birds and Bells and Pictures are not without a charm for me. I am a Seller of Soup, a Compounder of Hash, a Mixer of Mincemeat. And no Art of Musick will compensate for Badly Cooked or Meanly Served Food. But and if the Food is according to Hoyle, and each Bed is a Paid Up Insurance Policy against Insomnia, and besides this the Inn have a little Touch of Mystery and of Pleasant Memories, is that Idealism or is it Advertising?

And I said unto him. Thou art a Benefactor of Mankind. For thou hast made two Blades of Grass to grow where often there was less than one. Thou hast ministered unto a Physical Necessity in Exchange for Money, but thou hast contrived to touch the transaction with Poetry and Reverence. And the fact that thine Inn is now a Manifest Financial Success is one more proof that this old World is Fundamentally Sound at the Core; and that the things that are worth while have a little more than a fifty-fifty chance of success.

Being Put Off at Oconomowoc

The train whereon I rode was called the Olympian Limited. And I woke in the morning, and behold, the train was an Hour Late. And it troubled me not. For he who sold me my Ticket at Minneapolis said: This giveth thee a Ride unto Hartland, but a Sleep to Oconomowoc only. But and peradventure the Train be an hour or more late, so that thou miss the Local, then shalt thou ride on the Olympian to Hartland, and it will stop and let thee off.

So I woke, and said, I have an Hunch that I shall ride on this train to Hartland. And I went to sleep again.

And the Olympian stopped at Watertown Junction, and the Conductor spake unto the Porter, even unto the Ethiopian who ruled my Car, and said unto him. Waken up the man in Lower Six who hath a Ticket for Hartland, and put him off at Oconomowoc; for behold, we passed the Local back here at Astico, and he shall get off and ride on that. So shall this train not stop for him at Hartland.

Now I lay in my Berth and heard these words. Therefore did I not wait for the Ethiopian to tug at my Bedclothes, but I rose and put on my Raiment. And they put me off at Oconomowoc.

And the Local stopped at Giffords and at Okauchee and at Nashota and at Nagawicka. And then we came to Hartland. For the distance from Oconomowoc is Eight Miles, and there be Five Stops.

And as I rode I meditated, and I said. Upon that Train I was not Safed the Sage, neither was I any of the things wherein men might hold me apart from other men, but I was the man to be put off at Oconomowoc. And the Conductor thought concerning me only that he was mighty glad to get me off. And the men who gathered in the Washroom as the train drew nigh unto Milwaukee rejoiced that one man had gotten out so that he crowded them no more; even as the people give thanks in Rhode Island when a Fat man dieth.

And I considered the Train of Life, and those who ride upon it. I saw Thrones and those whose hands once held Scepters, but who now Saw Wood, and I said unto each of them: Here is where thou dost Get Off, for this is Oconomowoc.

I looked to the North, and I beheld Steel Strikes, and to the South, and behold. Coal Strikes; and to the East, and I beheld Police Strikes, and to the West, and there I saw Race Riots. Also I beheld them that worked with the hand getting great wages and they that worked with the brain sore pressed with the High Cost of Living. And I beheld in a Vision those that had been Masters moving into Flats, and they who had been Servants moving into Palaces; and they who had been rich hastening across the Street to a safe place on the Curb while they that had been poor Honked by and spattered mud upon them.

And everywhere was unrest and uncertainty. And it seemed to me that the Limited Train of Civilization was feeling the grip of new Brakeshoes on her Wheels, and that I heard the solemn tones of the Conductor, crying in a loud voice, and saying, Oconomowoc! All change.

The Man Who Ran Over A Rattlesnake

There was a man who owned an Automobile, and he drove unto places afar. And there was a day when he stepped on the Gas, and went out into the country. And he beheld in the road ahead of him a Rattlesnake. And the Rattlesnake was crossing the road, and asking of him no favors save that he observe the speed limit, and give unto Transverse Traffick a fair share of the Publick Highway. And when the man saw the Rattlesnake, he ran the wheels of his Car over it, so that the back of the Serpent was broken. And the Serpent writhed in pain and died and the man drove on. And he patted himself upon the back and said, I have wrought a good deed, and there is one less enemy of the human race. And that may have been true; neither am I reproving him for what he did; for I am no friend of Rattlesnakes.

Now it came to pass as he drove on, that one of his Tires went flat, and he stopped and removed it. And he found in the Inner Tube a small Puncture. For something had penetrated the Outer Tire, and cut it through. And he felt of the inside of his Outer Tire with his finger tips to find if peradventure a Tack had gone through his Tire, that he might remove it before he put in a new Inner Tube. And he found something that pricked his finger, and it felt like a Tack. But on the next day that man died.

Now I once knew the President of a Railway who was unjust to a Brakeman; and the Brakeman rose to be a Conductor, and then a Division Superintendent, and then a General Manager, and then he caused the President to be fired, and he sat in the President's seat and he said, It all was written down in the Book of Fate from the day the Old Man Cursed me from his Private Car.

And I have known of very humble men who have Resented being run over by Mighty Men, and who have kept it in mind for years until they found their opportunity. Yea, I have known the blind, unreasoning bite of a man whose back was broken to leave a poisoned fang for the finger of him who had run over him.

Wherefore beware lest thou think too meanly of him whom thou despisest; neither be thou too ready to run over even the humblest of the creatures of God. For in this manner are the haughty brought often to humility.

The Worm in the Concrete Gutter

There came a Heavy Rain, so that the Angle Worms did come out of their Holes in the Earth. And one of them wriggled over the Curb into the Street, and came into the Gutter. Now that street was Macadamized, and the Curb and the Gutter were of Concrete. And the Worm Wiggled along, and he was unable to Bore an Hole through the Concrete that he might find him an home in the earth; -neither could he climb again up the side of the Curb. And he was much Discouraged.

And I found him there.

And I said. This world is the world of a Good God, and in it every form of life hath some mission. I have read in a Learned Book how the Earth Worms like unto this one or its Ancestors did make this earth Fertile; else there had been no soil for the growth of such things as men do eat. And Worms are good also to feed the Early Bird, and to bait an Hook wherewith to draw out Leviathan. But where in all the providence of God is there moral meaning in the catastrophe of a Worm in a Concrete Gutter?

And I said, Little Worm, I have no present call to go a-fishing, and there is no early bird in sight. I might make an Hymn of thee, as certain men have done who call themselves Worthless Worms; but a man for whom Christ died hath no right to call himself a Worm; therefore will I cut out the Hymn Stunt, and call myself by a name either better or worse. But I have been in case like thee, where the Heavens were Brass, and the earth offered no refuge, and I should have been in Despair but for the Help of a Friend or the Love of God. Behold, I will be unto thee as God; for I have the power of life or death of thee.

And I picked up the Worm, and lifted him over the curb, and laid him on the Wet Earth.

And neither he nor the Early Bird knew that I had done this.

Even so hath God holpen me in times when I wot not of it.

Philosophy and Money

There came to me a Rich Man, who spake unto me, saying. What is a Philosopher?

And I said, As is his name, so is he; one that loveth Wisdom.

And he said. Art thou a Philosopher?

And I said. Humblest am I among the most humble of her servants; yet am I a lover of Wisdom.

And he said, I am no Philosopher, but I am a Rich Man. What dost thou consider a Rich Man to be?

And I answered, As one whom God hath blessed so richly with abundance of Soup whereon he filleth himself so that he hath no room nor appetite for the Ice Cream, so is many a Rich Man; but also there are Others. Of which sort art thou?

And he said. If thou art a Philosopher, thou shouldest know. But art not thou thyself a lover of Money? Yea, doth not every Philosopher love Money more than any Rich Man loveth Philosophy?

And I said. That question hath been asked of old. And there was a Rich Man in Olden Time who thus asked a Philosopher wiser than I. And that Philosopher answered, The reason that Philosophers care more for Money than Rich Men care for Wisdom is that Philosophers know what they Lack, and Rich Men know not.

And he said, The Philosopher who said that was a Wise Old Boy.

And I said, O thou Rich Man, thou art not altogether hopeless. Even like unto the Big Monsters of the Deep that yet are Mammals and not Fish, so hast thou something besides Gills; yea thou hast Lungs that are fitted for More Oxygen than thou canst extract from the Salt Water of Business; and now and then must thou Come Up to Breathe.

And I said unto him.

Hearken thou to me. The Philosopher is not saved by his Philosophy, and it is Right Possible for him to be at one and the same time a Philosopher and a Fool; neither is there any way under Heaven whereby either may be saved if he use not the gift of God for the welfare of others.

And he said. Thou art indeed a Wise Old Boy.

The Convention of the Lumbermen

The time drew on toward Christmas, and the ground was white with snow. And there came to the City where I dwell a Convention of Lumbermen. And they lodged in a great Inn, and they held daily Sessions, and they rode about the City, and had a Good Time.

And I attended one of their Sessions.

And there rose a man who owneth many Sawmills, and introduced a Resolution, denouncing the Habit of cutting down small trees for Christmas Trees.

And he spake on this wise:

Men and brethren, our craft is in danger. Behold how the price of Lumber soareth because the Trees grow few. Timber land which once cost us but few dollars an acre, now costeth us Many Dollars, and it lieth farther and farther from the Railroad. And what shall be the end thereof? Moreover, there are in this land Families unto the number of Twenty Millions, and each of them hath its Christmas Tree, which despoileth the land of its Young Trees, and cutteth off the supply of the Future. Wherefore, consider, and let us petition the Legislature to make it a Misdemeanor to cut down any tree for the purpose of making thereof a Christmas Tree.

And they spake one and another of them to the same end.

And I rose and said, O ye Strainers out of Gnats and Swallowers of Camels, before ye pass that motion, amend it so that it shall read that every Lumberman be sent to jail who cutteth down one large tree and planteth not ten small ones. Yea, and let him be beaten with many stripes if he leave his tops to take fire and burn over and desolate the land of its young timber. If thou wilt hang a few Lumbermen for their high crimes and misdemeanors, then will there be Lumber for all, and Wood to burn, and Christmas Trees once a Year for everybody.

And one of them said, Safed is an Idealist, but he knoweth not that the kind of lumbering which he adviseth is not Commercially Profitable.

And I said, Ye savers at the Spigot and Wastrels at the Bung, reorganize your business that it shall be profitable to provide for the Future as well as for the Present. And cease to condemn those who have small trees at Christmas.

And no man spake more in reply, but I inferred that my remarks were not Popular.

The Autumn Hollyhocks

There came unto me a woman, being unmarried, even one whom the profane call an Old Maid, being one of those women whom the Lord loveth too well to give her unto any one man.

And she sat before me in bitterness of spirit. And she said:

I desire to open unto thee mine heart, for it is full of bitterness. There is no one on earth to whom I am necessary. Behold, thine handmaiden was once young and fair, and when young men saw me, then did they desire me. And I might have been married and the mother of children. But my parents kept me close so that young men feared to look at me. And my brothers sought wives, and married and begat sons and daughters, and sent for me to take care of their children, but I had none of mine own. Yea, and when my father and my mother grew old, then did I remain with them, and care for them, and humor them when they grew Childish. And now they are dead and buried, and their souls are in Heaven, and my life work is done. And I am an Old Maid, and life hath nothing left for me.

And she said. If I go unto a Wedding, then do men whom I have known long, and who were young when I was young, joke with me, and say, It will be thy turn next. And I smile, though I fain would murder them. For being an Old Maid is no joke when one hath done her life work and hath more years to live and nothing to live for.

And I said unto her. The sun is bright, and the day is warm, for this is the season called Indian Summer; and for this and the Moccasin and the Canoe, I do thank the American Indian. Step out with me into the Garden, for I have somewhat to show thee.

Now the Garden was laid waste by the frost, and the beauty that had been was but a memory. But at one side is there a Mulberry Tree, and beyond it a Garage where I keep old books, and an Hoe and a Shovel and an Wheelbarrow: for I have no Automobile save an Wheelbarrow and the Cars of my friends, who are Many.

And under the shade of the Mulberry Tree, hard by the Garage, was there an Hollyhock in Full Bloom. And the color thereof was beautiful.

And she exclaimed concerning it, and wondered with great admiration that it was so late in Bloom, and the Blossoms so beautiful.

And I said unto this woman, even unto this Unappropriated Blessing who is called an Old Maid,

Thou art like unto this Hollyhock.

And she said, Do not mock thine handmaiden.

And I said, This Hollyhock was shaded by the Mulberry Tree and by the Garage, so that it grew slowly. But when the heat of the Summer fell upon the Garden, then did this Hollyhock grow secure and wilt not. And now when Frosts have fallen upon other Flowers, it blossometh like the Spring.

And I said unto her, Put on thy prettiest frock, and tire thine hair becomingly, and drop ten years from thine age, and go forth and blossom. For God hath yet work for thee even though thou live single. Yea, and because men are very Susceptible Creatures, who knoweth whether there be some Perfectly Good Widower looking for just such a Late-Blooming Flower as thou shalt be? And if not, still is it better to Blossom than to die with frost at the heart.

And the next time I beheld her, she looked ten years younger; and certain men did sit up and take notice.

And I counted this among my Good Deeds.

The Golden Hair

The daughter of the daughter of Keturah put her left arm around my neck, and drew my face close down beside hers, and held me where we could look both of us at ourselves in a large Mirror. And I saw therein the face of a dear little girl and the face of a Grandfather who loveth her.

And the little maiden appeared to see something and to miss something in what the Mirror disclosed. For she caught up her Golden Hair with her right hand, and cast it over my head.

And she cried out in great glee, and she said,

See, Grandpa, see. Your hair is Orange-Colored.

And I gave her a good, tight hug and a kiss. And I took her hand, and we came unto Keturah. And I said unto her. Who saith that Safed is Aged, and where is the man who doth affirm that his hair is Grey? Behold, mine hair is Red-Golden.

And I and the daughter of the daughter of Keturah showed unto her our Stunt. But we did not quite fool Keturah. For she knew what color was mine own hair that was underneath the golden curls of the little damsel.

Yet did I walk away with a lighter step, and I said, Let no man call me old. I have reliable information that mine Hair is Orange-Colored. I am not old, so long as I have a little Granddaughter to keep me young.

Now the season was the Autumn; for the summer was past, and the harvest was ended. And I looked at the Trees, and, behold, the leaves thereof were Red and Golden.

And I removed mine Hat, and I addressed Nature, saying,

I am something of a bluffer myself, and I understand thy Camouflage. Thou no less than I dost feel in thy veins the approach of Autumn, and thou makest a Brave Bluff. Thou canst not turn backward the procession of the Seasons, nor bind with the sweet influence of the Pleiades the flight of time nor the coming of the Frost. But thou hast somewhere hidden in the Woods a little Fairy that saith unto thee. Thou still art young; put on thy Glad Rags and Smile. And behold, here thou art, with Winter only two laps behind, and thou art pretending to feel young.

And I said,

Nature, thy method is O. K. and I am glad that out of the mouth of a little girl I have learned the same happy little Bluff. We are neither of us liars. Beneath every leaf that smileth as it prepareth to wither and to drop, is the bud of new life. The smile of the forest in Autumn is the prophecy within its roots of Eternal Youth. It is even so with me. It is not always May. But I am determined to keep my skyline clear and my waistline trim and mine heart young. And if ever I should have a suspicion that mine hair tendeth toward Grey, then I know how to change the color, and to go forth with head and heart both young.

The Little Girl in the Blue Dress

I rode upon a Train from New York even unto Chicago. And the Train was Full. And among the rest was there a Young Mother with a Little Girl. And they were going unto South Bend and the little damsel wore a Blue Dress.

And the little maiden and I became friends; for Little Girls like me, and I do verily believe that Good Little Girls are made of Sugar and Spice and all that is Nice.

And she had Dominoes wherewith to play. And she sat with me, and we set up the Dominoes to make Beds. And we made of them Single Beds, and Double Beds, and we tried to make Beds such as were in the Train, but we did not succeed very well.

And we had ridden all night and much of the day, and it drew toward evening. And I said, This place is Elkhart, and the miles unto Chicago are an

Hundred and One; and here do they cut off the Dining Car, and it is our last long stop. And we shall reach Chicago in Two Hours and Twenty Minutes, and South Bend will be before that.

And she said, I would that South Bend were farther.

And I inquired of her why she said so.

And she said. There will be Very Hard Letters to learn in South Bend.

And I said, Why dost thou think there will be Hard Letters to learn?

And she said, I had just begun to go to school when my father got a new job in South Bend and sent for us. And I learned A and B and C all the way down to X and Y and Z, and how to spell CAT and DOG and COW and many more. And my mother says that now I must begin all over again. And the Letters will be different; and who knoweth how they spell COW in South Bend?

And I said. Fear not. They spell it mostly with a C, and only a few of them begin it with a K.

And she said, It will all be so different, and I fear it. I wish this old Train would go on and on, and never come to South Bend.

And I saw that the little maiden was sore distressed by reason of the Very Hard Letters.

And I said unto her. Fear not, my dear. I have been in South Bend; yea, I have passed through it an hundred times. The letters there are A and B and C, and X and Y and Z, and there are twenty-six of them and no more.

And she inquired, Art thou sure?

And I said. Sure thing. And CAT and DOG are the same as in New York, and all that thou didst learn there will be good in South Bend.

And the little maiden was comforted.

Now this hooting, whanging train of human life moveth swiftly; and ever and anon there getteth on some passenger who wondereth how it will be in the place to which he journeyeth, and who approacheth life's destination with fear. And I prayed unto my God that he would send unto all such some of his Experienced Angels, who would say to all such timid souls, Fear not. The Alphabet of Heaven is the kindly deeds and gracious words which thou hast learned in the Kindergarten of Life. Heaven and Earth have a Common Alphabet, and all that thou hast learned will be of value there.

And the little maiden flung a kiss toward me as the Train pulled out of South Bend, and I beheld her in the arms of her father.

Seeing the Fire Engine

My little Grandson came unto my house, and he was Sobbing.

And I inquired, saying, Why is my little lad grieved?

And he burst into piteous Lamentation, and he cried, I want to see the Fire Engine.

And his mother spake, saying. We came past the Engine House, and the Firemen were Washing the Engine. And he desired to tarry, but I said. We will stop as we return from the Post office. And behold, when we returned, the Firemen had taken the Engine inside, so that we saw it no more.

There are sorrows great and sorrows small: but the sorrow of the small boy who hath desired to see the Fire Engine and hath not seen it is the Sorrow of Calamity.

And the little lad cried sore, saying, I want to see the Fire Engine.

And I said. Come with me, for we shall surely see the Fire Engine.

And as we started there came a man to see me, but I said, Tarry thou till I return, or come again another day, for I am busy.

And we went unto the Engine House. And I spake unto the Chief, and I saluted him, and he saluted me. And I said, We desire to see the Fire Engine.

And the Chief took the little lad and set him on high, so that he sat far up on the seat behind the Steering Wheel. And the Chief gave him the Bell Rope, and the little lad pulled the rope so that the Bell Rang.

And he saw the Ladders and the Truck, and the Chemical Engine, and the Whole Business.

And certain of the Firemen ascended the stairs, and slid down the Brass Pole that he might see how they descended when there was a Fire.

And the little lad had the Time of his Life.

Moreover, I had a Pretty Tolerably Good Time myself. For I am not too old to remember when I chased the Fire Engine.

So the little lad and I we came again, and I left him with Keturah, and with his mother the daughter of Keturah. And they said. Have you two Small Boys seen the Fire Engine?

And we answered and said. We have seen it. And my Grandson told about the High Seat and the Bell and the Brass Pole and the Chief.

Now it came to pass that night when I said my Prayers, that I spake unto Keturah, saying, Some good things have I done this day, and some it may be not so good. But one mighty good deed have I done: I let my work Go Hang for an hour while I went with the lad to see the Fire Engine.

For he who doeth a kind deed unto a little child, doeth it for all the long years that lie ahead of that young life. Wherefore do I say unto all men. Skimp not thy deeds of kindness to any sort of man or woman, but the good deed that lasteth longest is that which thou shalt do unto a little child.

And moreover, it is an Whole Lot of Fun.

The Wives of the Prophet

I and Keturah we were invited to a Reception. And Keturah inquired of me, saying, Which dress shall I wear? Shall it be my New one or my Blue one or the One I Wore Last.

And I said. Let it be the Blue one.

And she said, I will wear All Three.

For this is our Little Joke; and her New Blue Last Worn Dress looketh good unto me when Keturah hath it on.

And I said, There will be no woman there so fair as thou. For her Cheeks were red, and she stepped off as if she were Sixteen.

And she said, O my Lord, there is nothing more pleasing unto a woman than to look well in the eyes of the man whom she doth love. Nevertheless, I cannot forget the years nor the grey hair which the years have brought. God grant I may always look well in thine eyes.

And I said, Sure thing.

And I said. There was once a Prophet named Mohammed; and there are those who think that he was a False Prophet, but that concerneth not my story. And he had a wife whose name was Kadijah. And it came to pass after long years that she died. And he despaired of filling her place with any one woman, and he married many wives. And one of them was his Favorite, and her name was Ayesha.

And it came to pass that Ayesha inquired of Mohammed, saying. Am I not very beautiful? And he said. Yea.

And she inquired. Dost thou not love me? And he answered. Yea.

And she said. Am not I thy Favorite? And Mohammed looked around to be sure that none of his other wives were listening in, and he answered, Yea.

And she inquired yet further, Dost thou not love me more than thou lovest any of thine other wives?

And again he looked around, and he answered softly, Yea.

And if Ayesha had been wise she would have stopped there. But there was one question which she wanted to ask more than all, and she made the mistake of asking it.

And she said, O Mohammed, thou great and noble man, dost thou not love me more than thou didst love Kadijah? For she grew old and had wrinkles and grey hair, and I am young and fair.

And Mohammed answered with a Great Oath, and he said,

Nay, by Allah! For she it was who first believed in me!

And I said unto Keturah, Though all the fair women in the world were placed in line, and I were led admiring down the length of it, yet would I find no one among them all who could create for me the memories of our struggles and anxieties and economies and our meager triumphs and our sweet and holy joys. Thou in thy New Blue Last Worn Dress art unto thy husband the fairest among women.

And Keturah said nothing, but she found my hand as we walked away together, and she gave it a little squeeze.

www.ingramcontent.com/pod-product-compliance
Lightning Source LLC
Chambersburg PA
CBHW051737040426
42447CB00008B/1177